D1614280

6-25-71

DEFINITIONS IN POLITICAL ECONOMY

Also in

REPRINTS OF ECONOMIC CLASSICS

By THOMAS ROBERT MALTHUS

An Essay on the Principle of Population [1872]
First Essay on Population 1798 [1926]
The Measure of Value [1823]
Principles of Political Economy [1836]

The Pamphlets of Thomas Robert Malthus [1970]

DEFINITIONS

IN

POLITICAL ECONOMY

BY

THOMAS ROBERT MALTHUS

[1827]

REPRINTS OF ECONOMIC CLASSICS

AUGUSTUS M. KELLEY · PUBLISHERS

NEW YORK 1971

First Edition 1827

(London: John Murray, *Albemarle - Street*, 1827)

Reprinted 1954, 1963 & 1971 by
AUGUSTUS M. KELLEY · PUBLISHERS
REPRINTS OF ECONOMIC CLASSICS
New York New York 10001

. . . .

I S B N 0 678 00018 2
L C N 65 32785

. . . .

PRINTED IN THE UNITED STATES OF AMERICA
by SENTRY PRESS, NEW YORK, N. Y. 10019

INTRODUCTION

The *Definitions in Political Economy* contains Malthus's review of economic doctrine, not developed with a broad conceptual sweep, but deliberately narrow, suited to the problem of terminological clarification. This narrow focus and emphasis on precision by a man of Malthus's intellectual temperament may well have been a response to contemporary critics who frequently accused him of inconsistency and looseness of thought.[1] Indeed, Malthus accepts to some extent the judgment of his critics by remarking in a footnote: "I am very ready to include myself among those political economists who have not been sufficiently attentive to this subject [of precise definition of terms]."[2] Alternatively, of course, we may

---

[1] DeQuincey in his review of Malthus's *The Measure of Value Stated and Applied,* roundly condemned Malthus for inconsistent use of terms. (*London Magazine,* December 1823, reprinted in DeQuincey, *Collected Works,* Vol. IX, London, 1897, pp. 32-36.) Torrens remarked: "It is a singular fact, and one which it is not improper to impress upon the public, that, in the leading questions of economical science, Mr. Malthus scarcely embraced a principle, which he did not subsequently abandon." (Quoted in Ricardo: *Works and Correspondence,* edited by P. Sraffa, Vol. VI, p. 202n.) Cf. also James Bonar, *Malthus and His Work,* (New York, 1924), p. 297. For a discussion of the effect of this vacillation on Malthus's influence during the Ricardian era, see Morton Paglin, *Malthus and Lauderdale: the Anti-Ricardian Tradition,* (New York: Augustus M. Kelley, 1961), chapter VI.

[2] *Definitions,* p. 202n. However, it should be noted that Malthus makes this admission after he has criticized most of his important contemporaries for improper definitions and usage of economic terms.

evaluate this remark as just a species of disingenuousness.

Although the *Definitions* is organized primarily around the meaning and usage of key terms in economics by individual authors, rather than on broad analytical questions, Malthus gives restricted or brief consideration to a fair number of theoretical problems, and develops his ideas on the measurement of value over time, aggregate demand, Say's law of markets, etc. We have here in miniature a series of commentaries of the kind Ricardo prepared in his *Notes on Malthus*. The *Definitions*, taken together with Malthus's long article on the Ricardian School published in the *Quarterly Review*[3] constitute Malthus's systematic evaluation of contemporary economic doctrine. A brief comparison of these two critical works reveals a shift in Malthus's outlook: The *Quarterly Review* article was written in the heat of controversy with the Ricardians (1823) and shows Malthus's reaction to the triumph of the opposition. This is further borne out by some letters of the period.[4] By 1827 when the *Definitions* was published,

---

[3] This is Malthus's review of McCulloch's book-length summary of Ricardian Economics prepared for the 5th edition Supplement to the *Encyclopedia Britannica*. (Quarterly Review, LX, January 1824.)

[4] See especially Malthus's letter to Sismondi, included in Ricardo, *Works and Correspondence*, Vol. VIII, pp. 376-77.

Ricardo was dead for four years and Malthus had to face critics such as Bailey who generally lumped him in the same class as Ricardo. It is not too surprising then to find that a fairly sympathetic treatment is accorded Ricardo's work, even though McCulloch is dealt with harshly, but one is not quite prepared to find Malthus actively defending Ricardo's consistency and on occasion such orthodox Ricardians as James Mill and DeQuincey.[5] However, the reason is clear: when grappling with Bailey's sweeping attack on the relevance of classical value theory, Malthus plays down his differences with the Ricardians and defends his erstwhile opponents against the reasoning which would submerge them all. After giving spirited support to a point in DeQuincey's *Templar Dialogues*, Malthus remarks almost apologetically: "I have already stated that I decidedly differ from Mr. Ricardo, and it follows of course that I differ equally from the Templar, in thinking that the value of a commodity may be correctly expressed by referring to the producing labor alone; but compared with the expression of value proposed by the author of the *Critical Dissertation*, it has a prodigious superiority." (p. 157) Then after a detailed

---

[5] Cf. the lengthy defense of Ricardo's measure of value, *Definitions*, pp. 176-84, and the support of James Mill, p. 143n. Malthus's defense of DeQuincey is on pp. 154-61.

defense of the basic soundness of the Ricardo-DeQuincey position compared to Bailey's relativism, Malthus justifies his own theory which had also come under Bailey's attack.

The idea of a shift in Malthus's outlook with respect to the nature of his opposition is also supported by the allocation of space in the *Definitions:* Bailey's attack on classical value theory requires a refutation of 78 pages, more than the space devoted to Say, Ricardo, and James Mill combined. The Bailey chapter is by far the longest in the book; it indicates that Malthus, who was not disposed to give lengthy consideration to the arguments of minor opponents, considered Bailey a principal contender in the intellectual arena.

A brief run-down on the coverage of the *Definitions* may be helpful. After a passing glance at the Physiocrats and a short review of a few basic terms in Adam Smith, Malthus launches into an evaluation of the Ricardian School. Ricardo, himself, receives respectful treatment: "Mr. Ricardo has conferred an important benefit on the science of political economy" (p. 23), but the same cannot be said for his disciples James Mill and McCulloch. Malthus fires some effective salvos at both, reserving his most penetrating sarcasm for the pseudo-logical simplification of Ricardian doctrine developed by McCulloch. Extended attacks are also directed against Say's law of markets, and the widespread classical tendency to regard money as a veil obscuring the fundamental economic phenomena. On this latter point, Malthus effectively shows how the elimination of money from the exchange process leads to the absurdity of the Say-Mill-Ricardo position on the impossibility of a *general* failure of demand, or a glut: "The hop-planter who takes a hundred bags of hops to Weyhill fair, thinks little more about the supply of hats and shoes than he does about the spots in the sun. What does he think about, then? and what does he want to exchange his hops for? Mr. Mill seems to be of opinion that it would show great ignorance of political economy, to say that what he wants is money; yet notwithstanding the probable imputation of this great ignorance, I have no hesitation in distinctly asserting, that it really is money which he wants, and that this money he must obtain, in the present state of society, in exchange for the great mass of what he has brought to market, or he will be unable to carry on his business as a hop-planter. . . ." (pp. 53-53) "What an entirely false view, then, does it give of the real state of things, what a complete obscuration . . . to represent the demand for shoes as determined by the supply of hats, or the demand for hops by the supply of cloth, cheese or even corn. In fact, the doctrine that one half of the commodities of a country necessarily constitute an adequate market or effectual demand for the other half, is utterly without foundation. . . ." (pp. 55-56) "It is quite astonishing that political economists of reputation should be inclined to resort to any kind of illustration, however clumsy and inapplicable, rather than refer to money. I suppose they are afraid of the imputation of thinking that wealth consists in money. But though it is certainly true that wealth does not consist in money, it is equally true that money is a most powerful agent in the distribution of wealth; and those who . . . attempt to explain the . . . variations of wages and profits by referring chiefly to hats, shoes, corn, etc., must of necessity fail." (p. 60 n.)

Malthus, in the *Definitions* emerges as a fairly skilled debater. He easily points up the flaws in Mill's attempt to resolve the difficulties in the labor-quantity theory of value which Ricardo himself found insoluble. And it is with no little condescension that he disposes of McCulloch's clumsy attempt to reduce the action of "natural agents" (meaning time in the production process) to labor inputs (pp. 99-109).

It is interesting to exhume McCulloch's newspaper, the *Scotsman*, which was always attentive to controversies in political economy, to find McCulloch's reaction to Malthus's attack. McCulloch was the leading Ricardian disciple of the time, but the long review of the

Definitions which he wrote in the *Scotsman* of 10 March 1827 does little credit to his reputation. After a few empty verbal maneuvers ("why not say a steam engine labors?"), he fills much of the space with personal derogation: "Whatever others may think of Mr. Malthus's late speculations, it is pleasing to observe that they have in no degree fallen in his own estimation. The book before us is intended to show that whatever has been done by others during the last 20 years has been ill done, and those who wish to study Political Economy in its purity, unmixed with error or alloy of any sort, must resort to the writings of Mr. Malthus. According to his own showing, he is the 'Absolute Wisdom' of Political Economists—the real Simon Pure."

Let us finally consider Malthus's chapter on Bailey's *Critical Dissertation on the Nature, Measure, and Causes of Value*. This chapter is probably the most interesting in the volume, at least in the sense that it represents Malthus's response to a new challenge. Whereas the other chapters offer mainly a recapituation or elaboration of opinions and issues presented earlier in other works, the argument of Bailey struck a new note for Malthus; it threatened to make meaningless a theoretical issue (the best approach to the measurement of value over time) on which Malthus as well as the Ricardians had lavished a considerable amount of intellectual capital. Malthus met the issue squarely, even though the Ricardians had somewhat more at stake in the dispute.

Bailey's legitimate complaint against classical value theory was directed against the Ricardian attempt to define value in terms of a physical input—quantity of labor-time—and in that way reduce value (a psychological concept) to an absolute physical unit, completely independent of the market valuational process. But quantity of labor also represented sacrifice, or pain, and hence a psychological, real cost theory was implied by the quantity labor theory of value; however, the relationship between the physical and psychological dimensions of the labor theory were not explored (but merely asserted) by Ricardo. Absolute or real value measured by labor inputs proved to be a dead end in the theory of value, and Bailey did a service to the science of economics by emphasizing the weaknesses of this approach.

What bothered Malthus, however, was Bailey's refusal to consider the measurement of value over time a legitimate problem. As Malthus readily admitted, no precise measure here was possible, but economists have always required that a comparison of prices over time be made, and the concept of index numbers was eventually developed to meet the problem. Malthus saw the need to distinguish between the change in the price of a basic commodity (say wheat) which was attributable to a change in the general price level, and the change that was the result of a change in the real cost of producing wheat compared to the average cost of producing a large sample of other commodities which Malthus referred to as the "general power of purchase." According to Bailey, "the only use of a measure of value, in the sense of a medium of comparison, is between commodities existing at the same time."[6] To which Malthus replied that one could approximately gauge changes in value over time by comparing "the general power of purchasing which a commodity possessed at one period with its general power of purchase at another period." (p. 165) In modern terms, this "general power of purchase" is approximated by converting an actual price series to a deflated (constant dollar) series, through the use of a general index of prices, so that the value of a commodity over time is expressed in dollars of unchanging purchasing power. By looking at this constant dollar price series, one can get a *practical* answer to the question which Malthus and Bailey were debating—namely, can one measure the change in the relative value of a good over time? The fact that the resulting answer had theoretical flaws, Malthus clearly recognized.[7]

---

[6] Quoted in *Definitions*, p. 162.
[7] *Ibid.*, pp. 170-76.

The *Definitions* is an argumentative tract which provides much information about Malthus's position vis-à-vis his leading opponents. But unlike the *Essay on Population*, the tracts on rent and the corn laws, and the *Principles of Political Economy*, it is not directly concerned with the great policy issues of the time, and hence its appeal is to a narrow, more knowledgeable audience conversant with the economic doctrines of the classical period. Therefore despite its compactness, it is not recommended as an introduction to Malthus; this is better gotten from the works mentioned above. The *Definitions* is a valuable work for those already familiar with the issues which it raises, and who can appreciate it as a late phase of the great debate which Malthus and the Ricardians had carried on for some twelve years before 1827. Finally, and perhaps most significantly, it offers us an early confrontation of classical economics with the emerging subjective utility critique of classical value theory.

MORTON PAGLIN

International Population and Urban Research
University of California, Berkeley
October 1963

DEFINITIONS

IN

POLITICAL ECONOMY.

DEFINITIONS

IN

POLITICAL ECONOMY,

PRECEDED BY

AN INQUIRY INTO THE RULES WHICH OUGHT TO GUIDE
POLITICAL ECONOMISTS IN THE DEFINITION AND
USE OF THEIR TERMS;

WITH REMARKS

ON THE DEVIATION FROM THESE RULES IN THEIR
WRITINGS.

BY THE

Rev. T. R. MALTHUS, A.M., F.R.S., A.R.S.L.,

AND

*PROFESSOR OF HISTORY AND POLITICAL ECONOMY IN THE
EAST-INDIA COLLEGE, HERTFORDSHIRE.*

LONDON:

JOHN MURRAY, ALBEMARLE-STREET.

MDCCCXXVII.

CONTENTS.

PREFACE.

THE differences of opinion among political economists have of late been a frequent subject of complaint; and it must be allowed, that one of the principal causes of them may be traced to the different meanings in which the same terms have been used by different writers.

The object of the present publication is, to draw attention to an obstacle in the study of political economy, which has now increased to no inconsiderable magnitude. But this could not be done merely by laying down rules for the definition and application of terms, and defining conformably to them. It was necessary to show the difficulties which had resulted from an inattention to this subject, in some of the most popular works on political economy; and this has naturally led to the discussion of certain important principles and questions of classification, which it would be most desirable to settle previously, as the only foundation for a correct definition and application of terms.

These are the reasons for the arrangement and mode of treating the subject which has been adopted.

DEFINITIONS

IN

POLITICAL ECONOMY.

CHAPTER I.

RULES FOR THE DEFINITION AND APPLICATION OF TERMS IN POLITICAL ECONOMY.

In a mathematical definition, although the words in which it is expressed may vary, the meaning which it is intended to convey is always the same. Whether a *straight* line be defined to be a line which lies evenly between its extreme points, or the shortest line which can be drawn between two points, there never can be a difference of opinion as to the lines which are comprehended, and those which are not comprehended, in the definition.

The case is not the same with the definitions in the less strict sciences. The classifications in natural history, notwithstanding all the pains which have been taken with them, are still such, that it is sometimes difficult to say to which of two adjoining classes the individuals on the confines of each ought to belong. It is still more difficult, in the sciences of morals and politics, to use terms which may not be understood differently by different persons, according to their different habits and opinions. The terms virtue, morality, equity, charity, are in every-day use; yet it is by no means universally agreed what are the particular acts which ought to be classed under these different heads.

The terms liberty, civil liberty, political liberty, constitutional government, &c. &c., are frequently understood in a different sense by different persons.

It has sometimes been said of political economy, that it approaches to the strict science of mathematics. But I fear it must be acknowledged, particularly since the great devia tions which have lately taken place from the definitions and doctrines of Adam Smith, that it approaches more nearly to the sciences of morals and politics.

It does not seem yet to be agreed what

ought to be considered as the best definition of wealth, of capital, of productive labour, or of value ;—what is meant by real wages ;—what is meant by labour ;—what is meant by profits ;—in what sense the term ' demand' is to be understood,* &c. &c.

As a remedy for such differences, it has been suggested, that a new and more perfect nomenclature should be introduced. But though the inconveniences of a new nomenclature are much more than counterbalanced by its obvious utility in such sciences as chemistry, botany, and some others, where a great variety of objects, not in general use, must be arranged and described so as best to enable us to remember their characteristic distinctions ; yet in such sciences as morals, politics, and political economy, where the terms are comparatively few, and of constant application in the daily concerns of life, it is impossible to sup-

---

* It may seem strange to the reader, but it is nevertheless true, that the meanings of all these terms, which had been settled long ago, and in my opinion with a great approach towards correctness, by Adam Smith, have of late been called in question, and altered.

pose that an entirely new nomenclature would
be submitted to ; and if it were, it would not
render the same service to these sciences, in
promoting their advancement, as the nomen-
clatures of Linnæus, Lavoisier, and Cuvier, to
the sciences to which they were respectively
applied.

Under these circumstances, it may be desirable to consider what seem to be the most
obvious and natural rules for our guidance in
defining and applying the terms used in the
science of political economy. The object to
be kept in view should evidently be such
a definition and application of these terms,
as will enable us most clearly and conveni-
ently to explain the nature and causes of the
wealth of nations ; and the rules chiefly to be
attended to may, perhaps, be nearly included
in the four following :—

First. When we employ terms which are
of daily occurrence in the common conversation of educated persons, we should define
and apply them, so as to agree with the
sense in which they are understood in this
ordinary use of them. This is the best and

more desirable authority for the meaning of words.

Secondly. When the sanction of this authority is not attainable, on account of further distinctions being required, the next best authority is that of some of the most celebrated writers in the science, particularly if any one of them has, by common consent, been considered as the principal founder of it. In this case, whether the term be a new one, born with the science, or an old one used in a new sense, it will not be strange to the generality of readers, nor liable to be often misunderstood.

But it may be observed, that we shall not be able to improve the science if we are thus to be bound down by past authority. This is unquestionably true ; and I should be by no means inclined to propose to political economists " jurare in verba magistri," whenever it can be clearly made out that a change would be beneficial, and decidedly contribute to the advancement of the science. But it must be allowed, that in the less strict sciences there are few definitions to which some plausible, nay, even real, objections are not to be

made ; and, if we determine to have a new
one in every case where the old one is not
quite complete, the chances are, that we shall
subject the science to all the very serious dis-
advantages of a frequent change of terms,
without finally accomplishing our object.

It is acknowledged, however, that a change
may sometimes be necessary; and when it is,
the natural rules to be attended to seem to be,

Thirdly. That the alteration proposed
should not only remove the immediate objections which may have been made to the terms
as before applied, but should be shown to be
free from other equal or greater objections,
and on the whole be obviously more *useful*
in facilitating the explanation and improvement of the science. A change which is
always itself an evil, can alone be warranted
by superior utility taken in the most enlarged
sense.

Fourthly. That any new definitions adopted
should be consistent with those which are
allowed to remain, and that the same terms
should always be applied in the same sense,
except where inveterate custom has establish-

ed different meanings of the same word; in which case the sense in which the word is used, if not marked by the context, which it generally is, should be particularly specified.

I cannot help thinking that these rules for the definitions in political economy must be allowed to be obviously natural and proper, and that if changes are made without attention to them, we must necessarily run a great risk of impeding, instead of promoting, the progress of the science.

Yet, although these rules appear to be so obvious and natural, as to make one think it almost impossible that they should escape attention, it must be acknowledged that they have been too often overlooked by political economists; and it may tend to illustrate their use and importance, and possibly excite a little more attention to them in future, to notice some of the most striking deviations from them in the works of writers of the highest reputation.

8

CHAPTER II.

ON THE DEFINITION OF WEALTH BY THE FRENCH
ECONOMISTS.

It will not be worth while to advert to the
misnomers of the mercantile system; but the
system of the French Economists was a scientific one, and aimed at precision. Yet it
must be acknowledged that their definition of
wealth violated the first and most obvious rule
which ought to guide men of science, as well
as others, in the use of terms. Wealth and
riches are words in the commonest use; and
though all persons might not be able at once
to describe with accuracy what they mean
when they speak of the wealth of a country,
yet all, we believe, who intend to use the term
in its ordinary sense, would agree in saying
that they *do not* confine the term either to the
gross raw produce, or the neat raw produce
of such country. And it is quite certain that
two countries, with both the same gross raw

produce, and the same neat raw produce, might differ most essentially from each other in a great number of the most universally acknowledged characteristics of wealth, such as good houses, good furniture, good clothes, good carriages, which, in the one case, might be possessed only by a few great landlords, and a small number of manufacturers and merchants ; and in the other case, by an equal, or greater proportion of landlords, and a much greater number of manufacturers and merchants. This difference might take place without any difference in the amount of the raw produce, the neat produce, or the population, merely by the conversion of idle retainers and menial servants into active artisans and traders. The result, therefore, of comparing together the wealth of different countries, according to the sense of that term adopted by the Economists, and according to the sense in which it is generally understood in society, would be totally different. And this circumstance detracts in a very great degree from the practical utility of the works of the Economists.

Chapter III.

ON THE DEFINITION AND APPLICATION OF TERMS BY ADAM SMITH.

In adverting to the terms and definitions of Adam Smith, in his "Wealth of Nations," I think it will be found that he has less frequently and less strikingly deviated from the rules above laid down, and that he has more constantly and uniformly kept in view the paramount object of explaining in the most intelligible manner the causes of the wealth of nations, according to the ordinary acceptation of the expression, than any of the subsequent writers in the science, who have essentially differed from him. His faults in this respect are not so much that he has often fallen into the common error, of using terms in a different sense from that in which they are ordinarily applied in society, but that he is sometimes deficient in the precision of his definitions; and does not always, when adopted, adhere to them with sufficient strictness.

His definition of wealth, for instance, is not sufficiently accurate; nor does he adhere to it with sufficient uniformity: yet it cannot be doubted that he means by the term generally the material products which are necessary, useful, and agreeable to man, and are not furnished by nature in unlimited abundance; and I own I feel quite convinced that it is in this sense in which it is most generally understood in society, and in which it may be most usefully applied, in explaining the causes of the wealth of nations.

In adopting the labour which a commodity will command as the measure of its value, he has not, as it appears to me, given the most conclusive reasons for it, nor has he in all cases made it quite clear whether he means the labour which a commodity will command, or the labour worked up in it. He has more frequently failed in not adhering practically to the measure he had proposed, and in substituting as an equivalent the quantity of corn a commodity will command, which, as a measure of value, has properties essentially distinct from labour. Yet, with all this, it must be acknowledged that he has generally used the terms labour and value in the sense in which they are ordinarily understood in society, and has, with few exceptions, applied labour as the measure of value in the way in which it may be made most extensively useful in the explanation of the science.

It has been sometimes objected to Adam Smith, that he has applied the term *productive* in a new and not very appropriate sense. But if we examine the manner in which this term is applied in ordinary conversation and writing, it must be allowed that, whatever meaning may be thought to attach to it, from its derivation, it is practically used as implying causation in regard to almost any effect whatever. Thus we say that such and such things are productive of the best effects, others of the very worst effects, and others are unproductive of, or do not produce, any perceptible effects ; meaning by these expressions, that some things cause the best effects, others the worst effects, others, again, cause no perceptible effects ; and these effects may, of course, apply according to the context, and the subject under discussion, to the health of the body, the improvement of the mind, the structure of society, or the wealth of a nation.

Now, Adam Smith was inquiring into the nature and causes of the wealth of nations ; and having confined the term *wealth* to material objects, and described human labour as the main source of wealth, he clearly saw the necessity of making some distinction between those different kinds of labour which, without reference to their utility, he could not but observe had the most essentially distinct effects, in directly causing that wealth, the nature of which he was investigating. He called one of these kinds of labour *productive*, or productive of wealth, and the other *unproductive*, or not productive of wealth ; and knowing that it would occasion interminable confusion, and break down all the barriers between production and consumption, to attempt to estimate the circumstances which might *indirectly* contribute to the production of wealth, he described productive labour in such a way, as to leave no doubt that he meant the labour which was so directly productive of wealth, as to be estimated in the quantity or value of the material object produced.

In his application of the terms *productive* and *unproductive*, therefore, he does not seem to have violated the usage of common conversation and writing ; and it appears to me, that, if we fully and impartially consider the consequences of making no distinction between different kinds of labour, we must feel the conviction that the terms which he has adopted are pre-eminently useful for the purpose to which they are applied—that is, to enable him to explain, intelligibly and satisfactorily, the causes of the wealth of different nations, according to the ordinary meaning which men attach to the term wealth, whatever may be their theories on the subject.

Where Adam Smith has most failed in the use of his terms, is in the application of the word *real*. The *real* value of a commodity he distinctly and repeatedly states to be the quantity of *labour* which it will command, in contradistinction to its nominal value, that is, its value in money, or any other specific commodity named. But while he is thus using the word real, in this sense, he applies it to wages in a totally different sense, and says, that the *real* wages of labour are the necessaries and conveniencies of life which the money received by the labourer will enable him to command. Now, it must be allowed that both these modes of applying the word *real*, cannot be correct, or consistent with each other. If the value of labour varies continually with the varying quantity of the necessaries and conveniencies of life which it will command, it is completely inconsistent to bring it forward as a measure of real value. And if it can, with propriety, be brought forward as a measure of the real value of commodities, it follows necessarily that the average value of a given quantity of labour, of a given description, can

never be considered as in the slightest degree
affected by the varying quantity of commodities for which it will exchange. Of this Adam
Smith seemed to be fully aware in the fifth
chapter of his first book, where he says distinctly, that when more or less goods are
given in exchange for labour, it is the goods
that vary, not the labour.

It is evident, therefore, that to get right, we
must cease to use the term *real*, in one or
other of the meanings in which it has been
applied by Adam Smith.

If the term had never been applied in political economy in a different sense from that
in which it was first used by Adam Smith,
there could be no doubt that it might be ad-
vantageously continued, and the expression
real value might answer its purpose very
well, and save any question respecting the
substitution of some other term, such as intrinsic, positive, absolute, or natural. But
as the term *real* has been very generally applied, by most writers, to wages, implying
the real quantity of the means of subsistence
and comfort which the labourer is enabled to

command, in contradistinction to his nominal
or money wages, the matter cannot be so easily
settled, and we must come to some determination as to which of the two meanings it
would be most advisable to reject.

Adhering to the rules which have been laid
down, it will probably be acknowledged that
the term *real*, when applied to the means of
obtaining something in exchange, seems more
naturally to imply the power of commanding
the necessaries, conveniencies, and luxuries of
life, than the power of commanding labour.
A certain quantity of wealth is something more
real, if the word real be used in its most
ordinary sense, than a certain quantity of labour ; and if, on this account, we continue to
apply the term real to wages, we must express by positive, absolute, intrinsic, or natural, what Adam Smith has expressed by the
word real, as applied to value : or it would be
still better if political economists would agree
in assigning a distinct meaning to the term value, as contradistinguished from price, whenever the value of a commodity is mentioned
without mentioning any specific article in which

it is proposed to estimate it, in the same manner as the price of a commodity is universally
understood to mean price in money, whenever
the term is used without referring specifically
to some other article.

If, however, it should be found that the
term *real*, in the sense in which it is first and
most frequently applied by Adam Smith, has
by usage got such fast hold of this meaning,
that it cannot easily be displaced ; and, further,
if it be thought that an adjunct of this kind to
the term value will sometimes be wanted in
explanations, and that to express what Adam
Smith means, the term real is preferable to
either of the terms intrinsic, positive, absolute, or natural, there would be little objection to letting it retain its first meaning, provided we took care not to use it in application
to the wages of labour, as implying the necessaries, conveniencies, and amusements of
life.   Instead of *real* wages, we must then say
corn wages, commodity wages, wages in the
means of subsistence, or something of the kind.
But the other change is obviously more simple,
and therefore in my opinion preferable.

Chapter IV.

APPLICATION OF THE TERM UTILITY BY M. SAY.

IT would lead me too far and into too many repetitions, if I were to go through the principal definitions of the continental political economists, and examine the manner in which they have used their terms in reference to the obvious rules above laid down ; but I cannot resist noticing one very signal deviation from them in the justly distinguished work of **M.** Say. It relates to the term *utility.*

It must be allowed by those who are acquainted with **M.** Say's work, first, that he has used the term utility in a sense totally different from that in which it is used in common conversation, and in the language of those who are considered as the best authorities in political economy. Proceeding upon the principle, that nothing can be valuable which is not useful to some person or other, he has strangely identified utility and value, and made the utility of a commodity proportionate to its value, although the custom is universal óf distinguishing between that which is useful and that which is merely high-priced, of that which is calculated to satisfy the acknowledged and general wants of mankind, and that which may be only calculated to satisfy the capricious tastes of a few. He has thus violated the first and most obvious rule for the use of terms.

Secondly, he has gone directly against the usage of the best writers in political economy, and particularly against the authority of Adam Smith, whom he himself considers as the main founder of the science. Adam Smith has declared his opinion in the most decided manner on this subject, by contrasting value in use, and value in exchange, and illustrating the distinction between them by adducing the marked instances of a diamond and water. M. Say, therefore, in the manner in which he has applied the term utility, has violated the second obvious rule for the use of terms, as well as the first.

Thirdly, the objections to the old terms in

use, wealth and value, if there were any, do
not by any means seem to have been such as
to warrant the introduction of a new term.
The object of M. Say seems to have been to
show, that production does not mean production of new matter in the universe, but I cannot believe that even the Economists had this
idea ; and it is quite certain that Adam Smith's
definition of production completely excludes it.
"There is one sort of labour," he says, " which
adds to the value of the subject on which it is
bestowed * * * and as it produces a value may
be called productive."* There is, certainly, no
question here about the creation of new matter. And as M. Say observes, that when things
are in their ordinary and natural state their
value is the measure of their utility, while he
had before affirmed that riches were in proportion to value,† it is difficult to conceive what
beneficial purpose he could have in view in
introducing the term utility thus made synonymous with value or riches.

* Wealth of Nations, b. ii. c. iii. p. i. vol. ii. 6th ed.
† Traité d' Economie Politique, liv. i. c. i. pp. 2, 4,
4th ed.

Fourthly, as the terms useful and utility are in such very common use, when applied in their accustomed sense, and cannot easily be supplied by others, it is extremely difficult to confine their application to the new sense proposed by M. Say. It is scarcely possible not to use them sometimes, as M. Say himself has done, according to their ordinary acceptation ; but this necessarily introduces uncertainty and obscurity into the language of political economy.

M. Say had before made little or no distinction between riches and value, two terms which Mr. Ricardo justly considers as essentially different. He then introduces another term, utility, which, as he applies it, can hardly be distinguished from either of the others. The new term, therefore, could not have been called for ; and it must be allowed that the use of it in the sense proposed, violates all the most obvious rules for the introduction of a new term into any science.

Chapter V.

ON THE DEFINITION AND APPLICATION OF TERMS BY MR. RICARDO.

Although it must be allowed that the criterion of value which Mr. Ricardo has endeavoured to establish is an incomplete one, yet I cannot but think that he has conferred an important benefit on the science of political economy, by drawing a marked line of distinction between riches and value. A difference had perhaps been felt by most writers, but none before him had so strongly marked it, and attached so much importance to it. He agrees entirely with Adam Smith in the following definition of riches: "Every man is rich or poor according to the degree in which he can afford to enjoy the necessaries, conveniencies, and amusements of human life."* And adds an observation in which I think he is quite right. "Value, then, essentially differs from riches; for value depends not on

* Wealth of Nations, b. i. c. v. p. 43. 6th edit.

abundance, but on the difficulty or facility of production."* He subsequently says, " although Adam Smith has given the correct description of riches which I have more than once noticed, he afterwards explains them differently, and says that a man must be rich or poor, according to the quantity of labour which he can afford to purchase. Now this description differs essentially from the other, and is certainly incorrect; for suppose the mines were to become more productive, so that gold and silver fell in value, from the greater facility of production ; or that velvets were to be manufactured by so much less labour than before, that they fell to half their former value ; the riches of all those who purchased these commodities would be increased ; one man might increase the quantity of his plate, another might buy double the quantity of velvet ; but with the possession of this additional plate and velvet, they could employ no more labour than before, because, as the exchangeable value of velvet and of plate would be lowered, they must part with pro-

* Polit. Econ. c. xx. p. 320. 3rd Edit.

portionably more of these species of riches to purchase a day's labour. Riches then cannot be estimated by the quantity of labour which they will purchase."*

In these remarks I entirely agree with Mr. Ricardo. If riches consist of the necessaries, conveniencies, and luxuries of life, and the same quantity of labour will at different times, and under different circumstances, produce a very different quantity of the necessaries, conveniencies, and luxuries of life, then it is quite clear that the power of commanding labour, and the power of commanding the necessaries, conveniencies and luxuries of life are essentially distinct. One, in fact, is a description of value, and the other of wealth.

But though Mr. Ricardo has fully succeeded in showing that Adam Smith was incorrect in

* Polit. Econ. c. xx. p. 326. 3rd edit.—It may be remarked, by the way, that Mr. Ricardo here uses labour as a measure of value in the sense in which I think it ought always to be used, and not according to his own theory. He measures the exchangeable value of the plate and velvet, not by the quantity of labour worked up in them, but by the quantity they will command or employ.

confounding wealth and value, even according to his own descriptions of them ; yet he has nowhere succeeded in making out the propriety of that peculiar view of value which forms the most prominent feature of his work. He has not confined himself to the assertion, that what he calls the value of a commodity is determined by the quantity of labour worked up in it; but he states, in substance, the following proposition, that commodities exchange with each other according to the quantity of manual labour worked up in them, including the labour worked up in the materials and tools consumed in their production, as well as that which is more immediately employed.*

Now this proposition is contradicted by universal experience. The slightest observation will serve to convince us, that after making all the required allowances for temporary deviations from the natural and ordinary course of things, the class of commodities subject to this law of exchange is most extremely confined, while the classes, not subject to it, embrace the great mass of commodities.

* Polit. Econ. c. i. sec. iii. pp. 16, 18, 3rd edit.

Mr. Ricardo, indeed, himself admits of considerable exceptions to his rule; but if we
examine the classes which come under his
exceptions, that is, where the quantities of
fixed capital employed are different and of
different degrees of duration, and where the
periods of the returns of the circulating capital
employed are not the same, we shall find that
they are so numerous, that the rule may be
considered as the exception, and the exceptions the rule.

Yet, notwithstanding these admissions, he
proceeds with his rule as if there had been
few or no exceptions to it : he especially estimates the value of wages by the quantity of
human labour worked up in them ; and as it is
quite true, that if we look only to this element
of value, the value of wages has a tendency to
rise in the progress of cultivation and improvement, he has attributed the fall of profits which
usually takes place in rich countries to the
rise in the value of wages ; and, in fact, has
founded his whole theory of profits, which has
been considered as the crowning achievement
in the science, upon the rise and fall in the

value of wages. " It has been my endeavour," he says, " to show throughout this work, that the rate of profits can never be increased but by a fall of wages."* Again he observes, " Profits—it cannot be too often repeated— depend on wages ; not on nominal but real wages ; not on the number of pounds which may be annually paid to the labourer, but on the number of days' work necessary to obtain these pounds."†

Real wages, then, according to Mr. Ricardo's definition, are determined by the quantity of labour worked up in the articles, which the labourer receives as a remuneration for his labour, whether food and clothing, or money.

Now the meaning here attached to the term real wages, on which Mr. Ricardo's theory of profits is made to depend, is quite unusual, and decidedly contradicts all the most obvious rules which suggest themselves for the application of terms in any science.

In the first place, no one we believe ever heard, before the time of Mr. Ricardo, this

* Polit. Econ. c. vii. p. 137, 3rd edit.
† Id. p. 152.

term used in conversation in such a manner, that an increase of real wages would generally imply a diminution in the means of subsistence and comfort among the labouring classes and their families. Yet this would be the case, according to the sense in which Mr. Ricardo uses the term. Speaking of the different situations of the landlord and the labourer, in the progress of society, after describing the increasing wealth of the landlord, he says, " The fate of the labourer will be less happy; he will receive more money-wages it is true, (and the money of Mr. Ricardo is here used as measuring what he calls real wages ;) but his corn wages will be reduced ; and not only his command of corn, but his general condition will be deteriorated." With a continued increase of real wages, " the condition of the labourer will generally decline, while the condition of the landlord will always be improved."*

Secondly, No writer that I have met with, anterior to Mr. Ricardo, ever used the term wages, or real wages, as implying proportions.

* Polit. Econ. c. v. p. 98, 3rd edit.

Profits, indeed, imply proportions ; and the rate of profits had always justly been estimated by a per centage upon the value of the advances. But wages had uniformly been considered as rising or falling, not according to any *proportion* which they might bear to the whole produce obtained by a certain quantity of labour, but by the greater or smaller quantity of any particular produce received by the labourer, or by the greater or smaller power which such produce would convey, of commanding the necessaries and conveniencies of life. Adam Smith in particular had often used the term *real wages*, and always in the most natural sense possible, as implying the necessaries and conveniencies of life, which, according to the common language and feelings of men, might justly be considered as more *real* than money, or any other particular article in which the labourer might be paid. And the use of the term, in this sense, by Adam Smith, and most other political economists, necessarily made the new interpretation given to it more strange, and more unwarranted.

Thirdly, There were no objections to the sense in which the term was before applied. It was both natural and useful. Nor was a new interpretation of it wanted for the purpose of explanation. All the effects of the wages of labour upon profits might have been clearly described, by stating, that profits are determined by the proportion of the whole produce which goes to pay the wages of labour, without calling this proportion, whether small or great in quantity, *the real wages of labour*, and without asserting that, as the value of wages rises, profits must proportionably fall. That profits are determined by the proportion of the whole produce which goes to pay the wages of labour, is a proposition, which, when correctly explained, will be found to be true, and to be confirmed by universal experience ; while the proposition, that as the value of wages rises profits proportionably fall, cannot be true, except on the assumption that commodities, which have the same quantity of labour worked up in them, are always of the same value, an assumption which probably will not be found to be true in one case

out of five hundred ; and this, not from accidental or temporary causes, but from that
natural and necessary state of things, which,
in the progress of civilisation and improvement, tends continually to increase the quantity of fixed capital employed, and to render
more various and unequal the times of the
returns of the circulating capital.   The introduction, therefore, of a new meaning of the
term *real wages*, has not certainly the recommendation of being more useful.

Fourthly, the new sense in which the term
real wages is used, is not maintained with
consistency, or applied to old facts and opinions, with a proper allowance for the change
that has been made.   This is almost unavoid-
able, when old terms, which are quite familiar
in one sense, are applied in another and different sense.   It is particularly remarkable in
Mr. Ricardo's use of his artificial money, which
is meant to be the measure of real wages.
Thus, he says, " It may be proper to observe,
that Adam Smith, and all the writers who
have followed him, have, without one exception that I know of, maintained, that a rise in

the price of labour would be uniformly followed by a rise in the price of all commodities. I hope I have succeeded in showing that there are no grounds for such an opinion, and that only those commodities would rise which had less fixed capital employed upon them than the medium in which price was estimated, and that all those which had more would positively fall in price when wages rose. On the contrary, if wages fell, those commodities only would fall which had a less proportion of fixed capital employed upon them than the medium in which price was estimated ; all those which had more would positively rise in price."*

Now all these effects of a rise or fall in the wages of labour, depend entirely upon wages being estimated in Mr. Ricardo's imaginary money. Estimated in this way, and in this way alone, Mr. Ricardo's statement would be correct. But neither Adam Smith, nor any of his followers, down to the time of Mr. Ricardo, ever thought of estimating the price of wages in this way. And estimating them in the way to which they were always accustomed, that

Polit. Econ. c. i. sec. vi p. 45, 3rd edit.

is in money, as they found it, they are quite justified in what they have said. According to Adam Smith, at least, who estimates the value of commodities by the quantity of labour which they will command, if the money wages of labour universally rise, the value of money proportionably falls; and when the value of money falls, Mr. Ricardo himself says, that the prices of goods always rise.

The difference, therefore, between Mr. Ricardo and Adam Smith in this case, arises from Mr. Ricardo's forgetting that he was using the term price of labour in a different sense from that in which it was used in the proposition objected to.

In the same manner, Mr. Ricardo's very startling proposition respecting the effects of foreign trade, namely, that " no extension of foreign trade will immediately increase the amount of *value* in a country," arises entirely from his using the term value in a different sense from that in which it had been used by his predecessors.

If the value of foreign commodities imported is to be estimated by the quantity of labour

worked up in the commodities sent out to purchase them, then it is quite true that, whatever may be the returns, their value is unsus-
ceptible of increase. But if the value of foreign
commodities imported be estimated in the
way in which they had ever been estimated
before, that is, either in the money, in the
labour, or in the mass of commodities which
they would command when brought home,
then there cannot be the least doubt that the
immediate effect of a prosperous venture which
gives great profits to the merchants concerned
would be to increase the amount of value in
the country. The value of the returns compared with the value of the outgoings would,
in this particular trade, be greater than usual;
and it is quite certain, that this increase of
value in one quarter would not necessarily
be counterbalanced by a decrease of value in
any other. Practically, indeed, nothing is
more usual than a simultaneous rise in the
value of the great mass of commodities from
a prosperous trade, whether this value be estimated in money or in labour.

It must be allowed, then, that Mr. Ricardo

has been very far from cautious in the definition and application of his terms, in treating
of some of the most fundamental principles of
political economy; and I have very little
doubt, as I have stated elsewhere, that this is
one of the reasons why many of the readers
of his work have found great difficulty in understanding it.   When old and very familiar
terms are used in a new sense, it is scarcely
possible for the writer to be always consistent
in their application, and extremely difficult to
the reader always to be aware of the sense
meant to be affixed to them.

Chapter VI.

ON THE DEFINITION AND APPLICATION OF TERMS
BY MR. MILL, IN HIS " ELEMENTS OF POLITICAL
ECONOMY."

Mr. Mill, in his *Elements of Political Economy*, professedly lays no claim to discovery. His main object seems to have been to give the substance of Mr. Ricardo's work in a more concentrated form, and with a better arrangement; and this object he has accomplished. In the definition and application of his terms he nearly follows Mr. Ricardo; but it may be useful to notice a few cases, where he has either made the errors of Mr. Ricardo's definitions more prominent, or has altered without improving them.

On his first approach to the question of value, he describes the causes which determine it much more inaccurately than Mr. Ricardo. He says, that " the value of commodities is determined by the *quantity* of capital

and labour necessary to produce them."* But
this is obviously untrue and quite inconsistent
with what he says afterwards respecting the
regulator of value. It may be correct, and I
fully believe it is, to estimate the value of
labour by its *quantity ;* but how can we estimate the value of different kinds of machinery,
or different kinds of raw materials by their
quantity ? The *quantity* of raw material con-
tained in a coarse and thick piece of calico, as
compared with a very fine and thin piece of
muslin, worked up by the same quantity of
labour, may be four or five times greater, while
the value of it, and the degree in which it
affects the value of the commodity, may be
actually less. We cannot, in short, measure
the value of any product of labour by its bulk
or quantity ; and it must therefore be essentially incorrect to say, that the value of commodities is determined by the quantity of capital and labour necessary to produce them.

Proceeding afterwards to investigate more
minutely what it is, which in the last resort

* Elements of Polit. Econ. c. ii. sec. iii. p. 75,
2nd edit

determines the proportion in which commodities exchange for one another, he observes, that " as all capital consists in commodities, it follows, of course, that the first capital must have been the result of pure labour. The first commodities could not be made by any commodities existing before them. But if the first commodities, and of course the first capital, were the result of pure labour, the value of this capital, the quantity of other commodities for which it would exchange, must have been estimated by labour. This is an immediate consequence of the proposition which we have just established, that where labour was the sole instrument of production, exchangeable value was determined by the quantity of labour which the production of the commodity required. If this be established, it is a necessary consequence that the exchangeable value of all commodities is determined by quantity of labour."*

Now this necessary consequence, which is here so confidently announced, does not appear to me to follow either from this statement, or

* Elements of Polit. Econ. c. iii. sec. ii. p. 92.

from any thing which is said subsequently. Allowing that the first commodities, if completed and brought into use immediately, might be the result of pure labour, and that their value would therefore be determined by the quantity of that labour; yet it is quite impossible that such commodities should be employed as capital to assist in the production of other commodities, without the capitalist being deprived of the use of his advances for a certain period, and requiring a remuneration in the shape of profits.

In the early periods of society, on account of the comparative scarcity of these advances of labour, this remuneration would be high, and would affect the value of such commodities to a considerable degree, owing to the high rate of profits. In the more advanced stages of society, the value of capital and commodities is largely affected by profits, on account of the greatly increased quantity of fixed capital employed, and the greater length of time for which much of the circulating capital is advanced before the capitalist is repaid by the returns. In both cases, the rate at which commodities exchange with each other, is essentially affected by the varying amount of profits. It is impossible, therefore, to agree with Mr. Mill, when he says, " It appears by the clearest evidence, that quantity of labour in the last resort determines the proportion in which commodities exchange for one another."*

On the same grounds Mr. Mill is quite incorrect, in calling capital hoarded labour. It may, perhaps, be called hoarded labour and profits ; but certainly not hoarded labour alone, unless we determine to call profits labour. This Mr. Mill himself could not but see ; and consequently, in his second edition, he has deserted Mr. Ricardo, and boldly ventured to say, that " profits are in reality the measure of quantity of labour."† But as this very peculiar and most unwarranted abuse of terms belongs, I believe, originally to Mr. Maculloch, it may be best to defer the more particular examination of it, till I come to consider the definitions and application of terms adopted by Mr. Maculloch.

* Elements of Polit. Econ. c. iii. sec. ii. p. 94.
† Id. c. iii. sec. ii. p. 95.

In a work like that of Mr. Mill, which has so much the air of logical precision, one should have hoped and expected to find superior accuracy in the definitions, and great uniformity in the application of his terms, in whatever sense he might determine to use them ; but in this the reader will be disappointed. It is difficult, for instance, to infer from the language of Mr. Mill, whether a commodity is to be considered as altering in its value in proportion to its costs of production, or in proportion to its power of commanding other commodities, and they are certainly not the same.

At the commmencement of his seventh section, of chap. iii., entitled, " *What regulates the Value of Money*," he says,

" By the value of money is here to be understood the proportion in which it exchanges for other commodities, or the quantity of it which exchanges for a certain quantity of other things."

This is, to be sure, a very lax description of the value of money, very inferior in point of accuracy, even to what would be understood by *the general power of purchasing.* What are the things a certain quantity of which is here alluded to? and if these things change in the costs of their production, will money be proportionally affected?

But we have a different and better description of value in the next section. It is there said, that " gold and silver are, in reality, commodities. They are commodities for the attainment of which labour and capital must be employed. It is cost of production which determines the value of these as of other ordinary productions."*

Now, if cost of production determines the value of money, it follows that, while the cost of producing a given quantity of money remains the same, its value remains the same. But it is obvious that the value of money may remain the same in this sense of the term, while, owing to the alterations which may be taking place in the costs of producing the commodities alluded to, the quantity of other things for which it will exchange may be essentially different. Which of the two, then, is the true criterion of the value of money? It is surely most de-

* Sec. viii. p. 133.

sirable that the student in political economy
should not be left in the dark on this subject;
yet Mr. Mill gives him no assistance ; and he
is left to decide between two very different
meanings as well as he can.

But, perhaps, the most culpable confusion
of terms which Mr. Mill has fallen into, is in
relation to demand and supply ; and as he has
a more original and appropriate claim to this
error than any other English writer, and its
belief leads to very important consequences,
the notice of it is particularly called for.

In the first place, no person can have turned
his attention, in the slightest degree, to the
language of political economy, either in conversation or books, without being fully aware
that the term demand is used in two very
distinct senses ; one implying the quantity of
the commodity consumed, and the other the
amount of sacrifice which the purchasers are
willing to make in order to obtain a given
portion of it.   In the former sense, an increase
of demand is but very uncertainly connected
with an increase of value, or a further encou-
ragement to production, as in general the

greatest increase of such kind of demand takes place in consequence of a very abundant supply and a great fall in value. It is the other sense alone to which we refer, when we speak of the demand compared with the supply as determining the values and prices of commodities ; and in this latter sense of the term demand, which, perhaps, is in the most frequent use, an increase of supply is so far from increasing demand that it diminishes it, while a diminution of demand increases it.

Secondly, it has been generally agreed, that when the quantity of a commodity brought to market is neither more nor less than sufficient to supply all those who are able and willing to give the natural and necessary price for it, the demand may then, and then only, be said to be equal to the supply ; because, if the quantity wanted by those who are able and willing to give the natural price exceed the supply, the demand is said to be greater than the supply, and the price rises above the ordinary costs of production ; and if the quantity wanted by those who are able and willing to give the natural price fall short of the supply, the demand is said to be less than the supply, and the price falls below the ordinary costs of production. This is the language of Adam Smith, and of almost all writers on political economy, as well as the language of common conversation when such subjects are discussed. Indeed it is difficult to conceive in what other sense it could, with any propriety, be said, that the supply was equal to the demand, because in any other sense than this, the supply of a commodity might be said to be equal to the demand, whether it were selling at double or the half of its cost.

Thirdly, it must be allowed, that according to the best authorities in books and conversation, what is meant by the glut of a particular commodity is such an abundant supply of it compared with the demand as to make its price fall below the costs of production ; and what is meant by a *general* glut, is such an abundance of a large mass of commodities of different kinds, as to make them all fall below the natural price, or the ordinary costs of production, without any proportionate rise of price in any other equally large mass of commodities.

With these preliminary definitions, we may proceed to examine some of the arguments by which Mr. Mill endeavours to show that demand and supply are always equal in the aggregate; that an over supply of some commodities must always be balanced by a proportionate under supply of others; and that, therefore, a general glut is impossible.

If Mr. Mill had always strictly adhered to that meaning of the term *demand for a commodity* which signifies the quantity consumed, he might have maintained the position with which he heads the third section of his fourth chapter, namely, *that consumption is co-extensive with production.* This, however, is, in reality, no more than saying, that if commodities were produced in such abundance as to be sold at half their cost of production, they would still be somehow or other consumed—a truism equally obvious and futile. But Mr. Mill has used the term demand in such a way, that he cannot shelter himself under this truism. He observes, " It is evident that whatever a man has produced, and does not wish to keep for his own consumption, is a stock which he may give in exchange for other commodities. His will, therefore, to purchase, and his means of purchasing, in other words, his demand, is exactly equal to the amount of what he has produced, and does not mean to consume."*

Here it is evident that Mr. Mill uses the term demand in the sense of the amount of sacrifice which the purchaser is able to make, in order to obtain the commodity to be sold, or, as Mr. Mill correctly expresses it, his means of purchasing. But it is quite obvious that his means of purchasing other commodities are not proportioned to the *quantity* of his own commodity which he has produced, and wishes to part with; but to its *value in exchange;* and unless the value of a commodity in exchange be pro-

---

* Elements of Polit. Econ. c. iv. s. iii. p. 225. If the demand of every indvidual were equal to his supply, in the correct sense of the expression, it would be a proof that he could always sell his commodity for the costs of production, including fair profits; and then even a *partial* glut would be impossible. The argument proves too much. It is very strange that Mr. Mill should not have seen what appears to be so very obvious,—that supply must always be proportioned to *quantity*, and demand to *value*.

portioned to its quantity, it cannot be true that the demand and supply of every individual are always equal to one another. According to the acknowledged laws of demand and supply, an increased quantity will often lower the value of the whole, and actually diminish the means of purchasing other commodities.

Mr. Mill asks, " What is it that is necessarily meant, when we say that the supply and the demand are accommodated to one another? It is this (he says) that goods which have been produced by a certain quantity of labour, exchange for goods which have been produced by an equal quantity of labour. Let this proposition be attended to, and all the rest is clear. Thus, if a pair of shoes is produced by an equal quantity of labour as a hat, so long as a hat exchanges for a pair of shoes, so long the supply and demand are accommodated to one another. If it should so happen that shoes fell in value, as compared with hats, which is the same thing as hats rising in value, as compared with shoes, this would imply that more shoes had been brought to

market, as compared with hats. Shoes would
then be in more than due abundance. Why?
Because in them the produce of a certain
quantity of labour would not exchange for the
produce of an equal quantity. But for the
very same reason, hats would be in less than
due abundance, because the produce of a certain quantity of labour in them would exchange for the produce of more than an equal
quantity in shoes."*

Now, I have duly attended, according to
Mr. Mill's instructions, to the proposition
which is to make all the rest clear; and yet
the conclusions at which he wishes to arrive,
appear to me as much enveloped in darkness
as ever. This, indeed, was to be expected
from the proposition itself, which obviously
involves a most unwarranted definition of what
is meant, when we say that the supply and the
demand are accommodated to one another.
It has already been stated that what has hitherto been meant, both in conversation and
in the writings of the highest authority on
political economy, by the supply being accom-

* Elem. of Polit. Econ. c. iv. s. iii. p. 233.

modated to, or equal to the demand, is, that the supply is just sufficient to accommodate all those who are able and willing to pay the natural and necessary price for it, in which case, of course, it will always sell at what Adam Smith calls its natural price.

Now, unless Mr. Mill is ready to maintain that people would still say that the supply of a commodity was accommodated to the demand for it, whether it were selling at three times the cost of its production, or only one-third of that cost, he cannot maintain his definition. He cannot, for instance, deny that hats and shoes may be both selling below the costs of production, although they may exchange for each other in such proportions, that the hats produced by a certain quantity of labour may exchange for the shoes produced by the same quantity of labour. But can it be said on this account, that the supply of hats is suited to the demand for hats, or the supply of shoes suited to the demand for shoes, when they are both so abundant that neither of them will exchange for what will fulfil the conditions of their continued supply?

And supposing that, while both are selling below the costs of production, shoes should fall
still lower than hats, what would be the consequence?   According to Mr. Mill, " shoes
would then be in more than due abundance.
Why?   Because in them the produce of a
certain quantity of labour would not exchange
for the produce of an equal quantity.   But for
the very same reason, hats would be in less
than due abundance, because the produce of
a certain quantity of labour in them would
exchange for the produce of more than an
equal quantity in shoes."*

It will be most readily allowed that, in the
case supposed, shoes will be in more than due
abundance, though not for the reason given
by Mr. Mill.   But how can it be stated, with
the least semblance of truth, that hats would
be in less than due abundance, when, by the
very supposition, they are selling at a price
which will not re-purchase the quantity of labour employed in producing them.

Nothing can show more distinctly than the
very case here produced by Mr. Mill, that his

* Elem. of Polit. Econ. c. iv. s. iii. p. 234.

proposition or definition, which is to clear up everything, is wholly inapplicable to the question ; and that to represent the abundance or deficiency of the supply of one commodity, as determined by the deficiency or abundance of another, is to give a view of the subject totally different from the reality, and calculated to lead to the most absurd conclusions. There is hardly any stage of society subsequent to the division of labour, where the state of the supply compared with the demand of shoes is essentially affected by the state of the supply compared with the demand for hats ; and in the present state of society in this country, where the question of a general glut has arisen, it is still more irrelevant to advert to any other objects as efficient causes of demand for a particular commodity, except those which relate to the costs of producing it.

The hop-planter who takes a hundred bags of hops to Weyhill fair, thinks little more about the supply of hats and shoes than he does about the spots in the sun. What does he think about, then? and what does he want to exchange his hops for? Mr. Mill seems to

be of opinion that it would show great ignorance of political economy, to say that what
he wants is money; yet, notwithstanding the
probable imputation of this great ignorance,
I have no hesitation in distinctly asserting, that
it really is money which he wants, and that
this money he must obtain, in the present state
of society, in exchange for the great mass of
what he has brought to market, or he will be
unable to carry on his business as a hop-
planter; and for these specific reasons; first,
that he must pay the rent of his hop grounds
in money; secondly, that he must pay for his
poles, his bags, his implements, &c., &c., in
money; thirdly, that he must pay the numerous labourers which he employs on his
grounds, during the course of the next year,
in money; and fourthly, that it is in money,
and in money alone of all the articles brought
to the fair, that he can calculate his profits.

It is perfectly true, that both the landlords
and the labourers who are paid in money will
finally exchange it for something else, as no
one enjoys money *in kind*, except the miser;
but the landlord who may spend perhaps a

good deal in post-horses, dinners at inns, and
menial servants, would be little likely to ac-
cept from the hop-planter the articles which
he could get at the fair in exchange for his
hops; and though the expenditure of the labourer is much more simple, and may be said
to consist almost entirely in food and clothing,
yet it is quite certain that the power of commanding a given quantity of labour can never
be represented, with any approach towards
correctness, by a given quantity of corn and
clothing. As a matter of fact, the labourer
in this country is paid in money; and while it
often happens that for many years together
the money-price of labour remains the same,
the money-price of corn is continually altering,
and the labourer may, perhaps, receive the
value of twice as much corn in one year as
he does in another.

What an entirely false view, then, does it
give of the real state of things, what a complete obscuration instead of illustration of the
subject is it, to represent the demand for shoes
as determined by the supply of hats, or the demand for hops by the supply of cloth, cheese,

or even corn. In fact, the doctrine that one half of the commodities of a country necessarily constitute an adequate market or effectual demand for the other half, is utterly without foundation. The great producers who are the great sellers, before they can venture to think about the supplies of hats, shoes, and cloth, on which they may perhaps expend a tenth part of a tenth part of what they have brought to market, must first direct their whole attention to the replacing of their capital, and to the question whether, after replacing it, they will have realized fair profits. Whatever may be the number of intermediate acts of barter which may take place in regard to commodities—whether the producers send them to China,* or sell them in the place where they are produced : the question as to

---

* Foreign trade is, no doubt, mainly a trade of barter; but the question whether British woollens find an adequate market in the United States, does not depend upon their purchasing the same quantity of tobacco as usual, but upon whether the tobacco, or whatever the returns may be, will purchase the British money or the British labour necessary to enable the woollen manufacturer to carry on his business successfully. If both woollen manufactures and tobacco are below the costs

an adequate market for them, depends exclusively upon whether the producers can replace their capitals with ordinary profits, so as to enable them successfully to go on with their business.

But what are their capitals? They are, as Adam Smith states, the tools to work with, the materials to work upon, and the means of commanding the necessary quantity of labour. Colonel Torrens, therefore, is quite right, when he says, " that an increased production of those articles which do not form component parts of capital, cannot create an increased effectual demand, either for such articles themselves, or for those other articles which do form component parts of capital."* And, perhaps, he may be considered as making some approaches towards the truth, when he says, that " effectual demand consists in the

of production in money or labour, both parties may be carrying on a losing trade, at the time when the rate at which the two articles exchange with each other is the same as usual. This is the answer to the pamphlet, which M. Say addressed to me some years ago.

* On the Production of Wealth, c. vi. s. vi. p. 349.

power and inclination, on the part of consumers, to give for commodities, either by immediate or circuitous barter, some greater
proportion of all the ingredients of capital than
their production costs."*   But in this latter
position, he is still very far from representing what actually takes place.   When we
consider how much labour is directly employed
in the production of the great mass of commodities, and recollect further, that raw materials and machinery, the other two branches
of capital, are mainly produced by labour, it
is obvious that the power of replacing capitals will mainly depend on the power of commanding labour : but a given quantity of what
Colonel Torrens calls the ingredients of capital, can never represent a given quantity of
labour ; and consequently, if a given quantity
of labour be necessary in any production, a
very different quantity of the ingredients of
capital would be required at different times, to
occasion the same effectual demand for it.   It
is far, therefore, from being true, that if the

* On the Production of Wealth, c. vi. s. vi. p. 349.

ingredients of capital, represented by a hundred and ten quarters of corn, and a hundred
and ten suits of clothing, were increased to
"two hundred and twenty quarters of corn,
and two hundred and twenty suits of clothing,
the effectual demand for the article would
be doubled."*

It is still further from the truth, "that increased supply is the one and only cause of
increased effectual demand;"† and most happy
is it for mankind that this is not true. If it
were, how difficult would it be for a society
to recover itself, under a temporary diminution of food and clothing! But by a kind pro-
vision of nature, this diminution, within certain limits, instead of diminishing, will increase
effectual demand. The theory of demand and
supply, shows that the food and clothing thus
diminished in quantity, will rise in value; and
universal experience tells us, that, as a matter
of fact, the money-price of the remaining food
and clothing will for a time rise in a greater
degree than in proportion to the diminution

* On the Production of Wealth, c. vi. s. vi. p. 345.
† Id. p. 348.

of its quantity, while the money-price of labour may remain the same. The necessary
consequence will be, the power of setting in
motion a greater quantity of productive industry than before.*

There is no assumption so entirely fatal to
a just explanation of what is really taking
place in society, as the assumption, that the
natural wages of labour in food and clothing
are always nearly the same, and just about
sufficient to maintain a stationary population.
All the most common causes of an accelera-
tion or retardation in the movements of the
great machine of human society, involve va-

* It is quite astonishing that political economists of
reputation should be inclined to resort to any kind of
illustration, however clumsy and inapplicable, rather
than refer to money. I suppose they are afraid of the
imputation of thinking that wealth consists in money.
But though it is certainly true that wealth does not consist in money, it is equally true that money is a most
powerful agent in the distribution of wealth ; and those
who, in a country where all exchanges are practically
effected by money, continue the attempt to explain the
principles of demand and supply, and the variations
of wages and profits, by referring chiefly to hats, shoes,
corn, suits of clothing, &c., must of necessity fail.

riations, and often great variations, in the real wages of labour. Commodities in general, and corn most particularly, are continually rising or falling in money-price, from the state of the supply as compared with the demand, while the money-price of labour remains much more nearly the same. In the case of a rise of corn and commodities, the real wages of common day-labour are necessarily diminished: the labourer obtains a smaller proportion of what he produces; profits necessarily rise; the capitalists have a greater power of commanding labour; more persons are called into full work, and the increased produce which follows, is the natural remedy for that state of the demand and supply, from whatever cause arising, which had occasioned the temporary rise in the money-price of commodities. On the other hand, if corn and other commodities fall in money-price, as compared with the money-price of labour, it is obvious that the day-labourer, who gets employment, will be able to buy more corn with the money which he receives; he obtains a larger proportion of what he produces; profits necessarily fall; the capitalists have a diminished power of commanding labour; fewer persons are fully employed, and the diminished production which follows, is the natural remedy for that state of the demand and supply, from whatever cause arising, which occasioned the temporary fall in the money-price of commodities. The operation of these remedial processes to prevent the continuance of excess or defect, is so much what one should naturally expect, and is so obviously confirmed by general experience, that it is inconceivable that a proposition should have obtained any currency which is founded on a supposed law of demand and supply diametrically opposed to these remedial processes.

It will be recollected, that the question of a glut is exclusively whether it may be general, as well as particular, and not whether it may be permanent as well as temporary. The causes above mentioned act powerfully to prevent the permanence either of glut or scarcity, and to regulate the supply of commodities so as to make them sell at their natural prices. But this tendency, in the natural course of

things, to cure a glut or a scarcity, is no more
a proof that such evils have never existed,
than the tendency of the healing processes of
nature to cure some disorders without assistance from man, is a proof that such disorders
have not existed.

But to return more particularly to Mr. Mill.
After asserting that the supply is the demand,
and the demand is the supply, so frequently,
that the unwary reader must feel quite at a
loss to know which is which, he comes to a
distinct conclusion, which is so directly contradicted both by theory and experience, as
to shew either that his premises must have
been false, or that what he calls his indissoluble train of reasoning consists of mere unconnected links. He says, " It is therefore
universally true, that as the aggregate demand
and aggregate supply of a nation never can
be unequal to one another, so there never can
be a superabundant supply in particular instances, and hence a fall in exchangeable
value below the cost of production, without
a corresponding deficiency of supply, and
hence a rise in exchangeable value beyond

cost of production in other instances. The
doctrine of the glut, therefore, seems to be
disproved by a chain of reasoning perfectly indissoluble."*

While commodities are merely compared
with each other, it is unquestionably true that
they cannot all fall together, or all rise together. But when they are compared with the
costs of production, as they are in the above
passage, it is evident that, consistently with
the justest theory, they may all fall or rise at
the same time. For what are the costs of
production? They are either the quantity of
money necessary to pay the labour worked up
in the commodity, and in the tools and materials consumed in its production, with the
ordinary profits upon the advances for the
time that they have been advanced; or they
are the quantity of labour in kind required to
be worked up in the commodity, and in the
tools and materials consumed in its production
with such an additional quantity as is equivalent to the ordinary profits upon the advances
for the time that they have been advanced.

* Elem. of Polit. Econ. c. iv. s. iii. p. 234.

Now it surely cannot be denied theoretically, that all commodities produced in this
country may fall in comparison with a commodity produced in Mexico. As little can
it be denied theoretically that all commodities
produced by British labour may fall as compared with that labour, either from an unusu-
ally increased supply of such commodities, or a
diminution of demand for them. And when,
from these theoretical concessions, required by
the universally acknowledged laws of demand
and supply, we turn to the facts, we see with
our own eyes, and learn from authority which
there is no reason whatever for doubting, that
a very large mass of commodities does at
times fall below the costs of production,
whether those costs be estimated in money or
labour, without the slightest shadow of pre-
tence for saying that any other equally large
mass is raised proportionally above the costs
of production.

Even within the very last year, it is a matter
of the most public notoriety that the cotton
manufactures, the woollen manufactures, the
linen manufactures, the silk manufactures,

have all fallen below the costs of production,
including ordinary profits. To go no further,
the amount of these manufactures, taken
together, must, on a rough estimate, exceed
seventy millions of pounds sterling. And if
this mass of commodities, partly from over
production and over trading, and partly from
their necessary consequences, the shock to
confidence and credit and the diminution of
bills of exchange and currency, have fallen
below the ordinary costs of production, what
man is there credulous enough to believe that
there must have been, according to the language of Mr. Mill, " a corresponding deficiency of supply, and hence a rise of exchangeable value beyond cost of production
in other instances "?   I doubt, indeed, much,
whether satisfactory evidence could be brought
to show that a single million's worth of goods
has risen above the cost of production, while
seventy millions' worth have fallen below it.

Consequently, if the definition of a general
glut be a fall in a great mass of commodities
below the costs of production, not counterbalanced by a proportionate rise of some

other equally large mass of commodities above the costs of production, Mr. Mill's conclusion against the existence of a general glut, founded on " a chain of reasoning perfectly indissoluble," seems to be utterly without foundation.

If facts so notorious as these to which I have adverted are either boldly denied, or considered as undeserving attention, in founding the theories of political economy, there is an end at once to the utility of the science.

On the subject of the wages of labour, Mr. Mill has added his authority to the peculiar views and language of Mr. Ricardo. He says, " Whatever the share of the labourer, such is the rate of wages ; and, *vice versâ*, whatever the rate of wages, such is the share of the commodity or commodities' worth which the labourer receives."* Perhaps the term *rate of wages* used by Mr. Mill to express the proportion of the produce which falls to the share of the labourer is in some respects preferable to the term *real wages*, used by Mr. Ricardo for the same purpose ; but still it is highly

* Elements of Polit. Econ. c. ii. sec. ii. p. 41.

objectionable, because it is an old and familiar term used in an entirely new sense. When the expressions high or low rates of wages were used, before the time of Mr. Ricardo and Mr. Mill, no one understood them to mean the proportion of the produce awarded to the labourer. In fact, this meaning had not been before conveyed by any appropriate terms in the language of political economy ; yet it is a meaning the expression of which was much wanted in explaining the theory of profits. To express it, therefore, a new term should certainly have been chosen, and not an old one, which was familiar in a different sense. There seems to be no objection to the term *proportionate wages*, which has been used by Mr. Macculloch.

On the whole, it must be allowed, that Mr. Mill in his *Elements of Political Economy* has but little attended to the most obvious rules which ought to guide political economists in the definition and application of their terms. They are often unsanctioned by the proper authorities, and rarely maintained with consistency.

Chapter VII.

ON THE DEFINITION AND APPLICATION OF TERMS,
BY MR. MACCULLOCH, IN HIS " PRINCIPLES OF
POLITICAL ECONOMY."

However incautious Mr. Ricardo and Mr. Mill may have been in the definition and application of their terms, I fear it will be found that Mr. Macculloch has been still more so; and that, instead of growing more careful, the longer he considers the subject, he seems to be growing more rash and inconsiderate.

The expositors of any science are in general desirous of calling into their service definite and appropriate terms; and for this purpose their main object is to look for characteristic differences, not partial resemblances. Mr. Macculloch, on the other hand, seems to be only looking out for resemblances: and proceeding upon this principle, he is led to confound material with immaterial objects; productive with unproductive labour; capital with revenue; the food of the labourer with the labourer himself; production with consumption; and labour with profits.

That this is not an exaggerated view of what has been stated by Mr. Macculloch, in his *Principles of Political Economy*, any person who reads the work with attention may satisfy himself.

Mr. Macculloch's definition of wealth, which he considers as quite unexceptionable, is, " those articles or products which possess exchangeable value, and are either necessary, useful, or agreeable."*

It is not, perhaps, quite unexceptionable to use the term *value* in a definition of wealth. It is something like explaining *ignotum per ignotius*. But independently of this objection, the definition is so worded, that it is left in doubt whether immaterial gratifications are meant to be included in it. They are not in general designated by the terms *articles* or *products;* and it is only made clear that it is intended to include them by a collateral remark on my definition of wealth, which I confine specifically to material objects, and by a sub-

* Principles of Political Economy, part i. p. 5.

sequent definition of productive labour, which
is made to include every gratification derived
from human exertion.

Mr. Macculloch, in the article on Political
Economy which he published in the Supplement to the Encyclopædia Britannica, had
excluded these kinds of gratification from his
definition of wealth, and had given such reasons
for this exclusion, as would fully have convinced
me of its propriety, if I had not been convinced
before. He observes that, " if political economy were to embrace a discussion of the production and distribution of all that is useful and
agreeable, it would include within itself every
other science; and the best Encyclopædia would
really be the best treatise on political economy.
Good health is useful and delightful, and therefore, on this hypothesis, the science of wealth
ought to comprehend the science of medicine:
civil and religious liberty are highly useful,
and therefore the science of wealth must comprehend the science of politics : good acting
is agreeable, and therefore, to be complete,
the science of wealth must embrace a discussion of the principles of the histrionic art, and

so on. Such definitions are obviously worse
than useless. They can have no effect but to
generate confused and perplexed notions respecting the objects and limits of the science,
and to prevent the student ever acquiring a
clear and distinct idea of the inquiries in which
he is engaged."*

On these grounds he confined wealth to
material products ; but, in the same treatise,
he included, in his definition of productive labour, all those sources of gratification which
he had, with such good reason, excluded from
his definition of wealth. When he had done
this, however, he could not but be struck with

* These remarks were principally directed against
Lord Lauderdale's definition of wealth—*all that man
desires as useful and delightful to him ;* but they apply
with nearly equal force to Mr. Macculloch's present definition, which is limited to those objects which possess
exchangeable value. According to Mr. Macculloch's
own statement, health is purchased from the physician,
and the gratification derived from acting from the actor;
and it must be allowed that it is impossible to enjoy the
benefits of civil and religious liberty without paying
those who administer a good government. It has been
said by Mr. Hallam, with some truth, that the liberties
of England were chiefly obtained by successive pur
chases from the crown.

the inconsistency of saying that wealth con-
sisted exclusively of material products, and
yet that all labour was equally productive of
wealth, whether it produced material products
or not. To get rid of this inconsistency, he
has now altered his definition, by leaving out
the term material products; and it remains
to be seen, whether in so doing he has not
essentially deviated from the most obvious
rules which should direct us in defining our
terms.

His definition of wealth, as explained by
what he subsequently says of productive labour, now includes all the gratifications derived
from menial service and followers, whatever
may be their number.

Now let us suppose two fertile countries
with the same population and produce, in one
of which it was the pride and pleasure of the
landlords to employ their rents chiefly in
maintaining menial servants and followers,
and in the other, chiefly in the purchase of
manufactures and the products of foreign
commerce. It is evident that the different
results would be nearly what I described in

speaking of the consequences of the definition
of the Economists. In the country, where the
tastes and habits of the landlords led them to
prefer material conveniencies and luxuries,
there would, in the first place, be in all pro-
bability a much better division of landed
property; secondly, supposing the same agricultural capital, there would be a very much
greater quantity of manufacturing and mercantile capital; and thirdly, the structure of
society would be totally different. In the one
country, there would be a large body of persons
living upon the profits of capital; in the other,
comparatively a very small one : in the one,
there would be a large middle class of society ;
in the other, the society would be divided
almost entirely between a few great landlords and their menials and dependents : in
the one country, good houses, good furniture,
good clothes, and good carriages, would be
in comparative abundance ; while in the other,
these conveniencies would be confined to a
very few.

Now, I would ask, whether it would not be
the grossest violation of all common language,

and all common feelings and apprehensions, to say that the two countries were equally rich?

Mr. Macculloch, however, has discovered that there is a resemblance between the end accomplished by the menial servant or dependent, and by the manufacturer or agriculturist. He says, " The end of all human exertion is the same ; that is, to increase the sum of necessaries, comforts, and enjoyments ; and it must be left to the judgment of every one to determine what proportion of these comforts he will have in the shape of menial services, and what in the shape of material products."*

It will, indeed, be readily allowed, that even the third footman who stands behind a coach, and seems only to add to the fatigue of the horses and the wear and tear of the carriage, is still employed to gratify some want or wish of man, in the same manner as the riband maker or the lace maker. It will further be readily allowed, that it is by no means politic to interfere with individuals in the modes of spending their incomes. But

* Principles of Polit. Econ., part iv. p. 406.

does it at all follow from this, that if these different kinds of labour have very different effects on society in regard to wealth, as the term is understood by the great mass of mankind, that they should not be distinguished by different appellations, in order to facilitate the explanation of these different effects? Mr. Macculloch might unquestionably discover some resemblance between the salt and the meat which it seasons : they both contribute, when used in proper proportions, to compose a palatable and nutritive meal, and in general we may leave it to the taste and discretion of the individual to determine these proportions ; but are we on that account to confound the two substances together, and to affirm that they are *equally* nutritive? Are we to define and apply our terms in such a way as to make it follow from our statements, that, if the individual were to compound his repast of half salt and half meat, it would equally conduce to his health and strength?

But Mr. Macculloch states, that a taste for the gratifications derived from the unproductive labourers of Adam Smith " has exactly

the same effect upon national wealth as a
taste for tobacco, champagne, or any other
luxury."* This may be directly denied,
unless we define wealth in such a manner as
will entitle us to say that the enjoyments
derived by a few great landlords, from the
parade of menial servants and followers, will
tell as effectually in an estimate of wealth as a
large mass of manufacturers and foreign commodities. But when M. Chaptal endeavoured
to estimate the wealth of France, and Mr. Col-
quhoun that of England, we do not find the
value of these enjoyments computed in any
of their tables. And certainly, if wealth
means what it is understood to mean in common conversation and in the language of the
highest authorities in the science of Political
Economy, no effects on national wealth can
or will be more distinct than those which
result from a taste for material conveniencies
and luxuries, and a taste for menial servants
and followers. The exchange of the ordinary
products of land for manufactures, tobacco,
and champagne necessarily generates capital ;

* Principles of Polit. Econ., part iv. p. 410.

and the more such exchanges prevail the more do those advantages prevail which result from the growth of capital and a better structure of society ; while an exchange of necessaries for menial services, beyond a certain limited amount, obviously tends to check the growth of capital, and, if pushed to a considerable extent, to prevent accumulation entirely, and to keep a country permanently in a semi-barbarous state.

Mr. Macculloch, when not under the influence of his definition, justly observes, that " the great practical problem, involved in that part of the science of political economy which treats of the production of wealth, must resolve itself into a discussion of the means whereby the greatest amount of necessary, useful, and desirable products may be obtained with the least possible quantity of labour."* But among the unproductive labourers of Adam Smith there is no room for such saving of labour. The pre-eminent ad-

* Principles of Polit. Econ., part ii. p. 71. This language has absolutely no meaning, if all labour be equally productive in regard to national wealth.

vantages to be derived from capital, machinery, and the division of labour, are here
almost entirely lost; and in most instances the
saving of labour would defeat the very end in
view, namely, the parade of attendance, and
the pride of commanding a numerous body of
followers.

Now, if the employment of the labour required to produce material conveniencies and
luxuries necessarily occasions the creation and
distribution of capital, and, further, affords
room for all the advantages resulting from
the saving of labour and the most extended
use of machinery; while the employment of
the labour, called by Adam Smith unproductive, is necessarily cut off from all these
benefits, I would ask whether these two circumstances *alone* do not form a sufficiently
marked line of distinction amply to justify the
classification of Adam Smith; and the utility
of such a classification, in explaining the
causes of the wealth of nations, is most obvious and striking.

So difficult is it, consistently, to maintain
a definition which contradicts the common
usage of language, and the common feelings

of mankind, that I have not the least doubt,
if Mr. Macculloch himself were to travel
through two countries of the kind before
described, that is, one flourishing in manufactures and commerce, and the other, though
with the same population and food, furnishing
little more to the great mass of its people
than *panem et Circenses*, he would call the
latter poor, and the former comparatively
rich.

Now, what must have been the cause of
this difference? Adam Smith would give a
simple, sufficient, and most intelligible reason
for it. He would say, that the number and
powers of those whom he had called productive labourers, had been much greater in one
country than in the other. This seems to be
a clear and satisfactory explanation. How
Mr. Macculloch could explain the matter
according to doctrines which make no difference between the different kinds of labour,
I am utterly at a loss to conjecture*.

---

* Mr. Macculloch dwells very much upon the extreme importance of accumulation to the increase of
national wealth. But how are the gratifications afforded
by menial servants to be accumulated?

Perhaps, however, he would say, upon re-
collection, that his definition of wealth did not
oblige him to allow that there would really
be any difference in the wealth of these two
countries. In that case, I think it may be
very safely said that his definition of wealth
violates all the most obvious rules for the
definition and application of terms. It is opposed to the meaning of the term wealth as
used in common conversation; it is opposed
to the meaning of the term wealth as applied
by the writers of the highest authority in
political economy; it is so far from removing
the little difficulties which had attended
former definitions of wealth and productive
labour, that it very greatly aggravates them;
it so contradicts our common habits and feelings, that it is scarcely possible to maintain it
with consistency.

Mr. Macculloch's definition of capital has
exactly the same kind of character as his definition of wealth, namely, that of being so
extended as to destroy all precision, and to
confound objects which had before been most
usefully separated, with a view to the expla-

nation of the causes of the wealth of nations. The alteration of a definition seems with Mr. Macculloch to be a matter of very slight consequence. The following passage is certainly a most extraordinary one. " The capital of a country may be defined to be *that portion of the produce of industry existing in it, which can be made directly available, either to the support of human existence, or to the facilitating of production.* This definition differs from that given by Dr. Smith, which has been adopted by most other economists. The whole produce of industry belonging to a country, is said to form its *stock ;* and its capital is supposed to consist of that portion only of its stock, which is employed in the view of producing some species of commodities. The other portion of the stock of a country, or that which is employed to maintain its inhabitants, without any immediate view to production, has been denominated its *revenue,* and is not supposed to contribute anything to the increase of its wealth."

" These distinctions seem to rest on no good foundations. Portions of stock employed without any immediate view to production, are often by far the most productive. The stock, for example, that Arkwright and Watt employed in their own consumption, and without which they could not have subsisted, was laid out as *revenue;* and yet it is quite certain that it contributed infinitely more to increase their own wealth, as well as that of the country, than any equal quantity of stock expended on the artisans in their service. It is always extremely difficult to say whether any portion of stock is, or is not, productively employed; and any definition of capital which involves the determination of this point, can only serve to embarrass and obscure a subject that is otherwise abundantly simple. In our view of the matter, it is enough to constitute an article capital, if it can either directly contribute to the support of man, or assist him in appropriating or producing commodities ; but the question respecting the mode of employing an article ought certainly to be held to be, what it obviously is, perfectly distinct from the question whether that article is capital. For any thing that we can *à priori* know to

the contrary, a horse yoked to a gentleman's
coach may be just as productively employed
as if he were yoked to a brewer's dray, though
it is quite plain, that whatever difference may
really obtain in the two cases, the identity of
the horse is not affected ; he is equally possessed, in the one case as well as the other,
of the capacity to assist in production, and
so long as he possesses that capacity, he
ought to be viewed, independently of all other
considerations, as a portion of the capital of
the country."*

If these doctrines were admitted, there
would be an end, at once, of all classifications,
and of all those appropriate designations
which so essentially assist us, in explaining
what is going forward in society.   If the distinction between the whole mass of the products of a country, and those parts of it which
are applied to perform particular functions,
rests on no solid foundation, it may be asked,
on what better foundation does the distinction
between the mass of the male population of a
country, and the classes of lawyers, physicians,

* Principles of Polit. Econ., part ii. p. 92.

manufacturers, and agriculturists rest? They
all equally come under the general denomination of men ; but particular classes are
most usefully distinguished by particular appellations founded on the particular functions
which they generally perform.

The bread which I consume myself, or give
to a menial servant, is a part of the general
produce of the country, and may not be different from that which is advanced to a manufacturer or agriculturist. When I or my
servant consume the bread, it performs a
most necessary and important service, no less
than the maintenance of life and health ; but
in obtaining this service my wealth is *pro
tanto* diminished. On the other hand, if I
give the same kind of bread as wages to a
manufacturer or agricultural labourer, it will
not, with regard to me, perform so necessary
an office as before, but it will perform an
essentially different one with regard to my
wealth, it will increase my wealth instead of
diminishing it. In an inquiry into the causes
of the wealth of nations, does not this differ-

ence in the functions which the same advances perform require to be marked by a particular appellation?

Accordingly, both in the language of common conversation and of the best writers, revenue and capital have always been distinguished; by revenue being understood, that which is expended with a view to immediate support and enjoyment, and by capital, that which is expended with a view to profit. But in the language of Mr. Macculloch, in the passage above quoted, it is the capacity to perform particular functions, and not the habitual performance of them, that justifies particular designations. A coach-horse, drawing a chariot in the Park, has the capacity of being employed in a brewer's dray or a farmer's waggon : " whatever difference may really obtain in the two cases, the identity of the horse is not affected; he is equally possessed, in the one case as in the other, of the capacity to assist in production; and so long as he possesses that capacity, he ought to be viewed, independently of all other considerations, as a portion of the capital of the country."

This appears to me to be very little different from saying that a man who is capable of being made to perform the functions of a judge ought to be denominated a judge ; because, whether he sits on the bench or in the court below, the identity of the man is the same ; he is equally possessed, in the one case as well as the other, of the capacity to assist in the decision of causes, and so long as he possesses that capacity he ought to be viewed, independently of all other considerations, as one of the judges of the country. It is said, that the French are astonished at the small number of judges in England. If this kind of comprehensive nomenclature were adopted, their wonder would soon cease.

The whole of the incomes of every person in a society, in whatever way they may be actually employed, might be employed, as far as they would go, directly in the support of man. Consequently, according to the definitions of Mr. Macculloch, all incomes are capital. But he is not satisfied even with this very unusually-extended meaning of the term. He can trace a resemblance between a working man and a working horse, and is, consequently, led to say, " However extended the sense previously attached to the term capital may at first sight appear, I am satisfied that it ought to be interpreted still more comprehensively. Instead of understanding by capital all that portion of the produce of industry extrinsic to man, which may be applicable to his support, and to the facilitating of production, there does not seem to be any good reason why man himself should not, and very many why he should, be considered as forming a part of the national capital. Man is as much the produce of labour as any of the machines constructed by his agency ; and it appears to us, that in all economical investigations he ought to be considered in precisely the same point of view."*

That there is some resemblance between a

* Principles of Polit. Econ., part ii. p. 114.

working man and a working horse cannot for
a moment be doubted ; but is that sufficient
reason why they should be confounded together under the name of capital ? The question
is not whether there is a partial resemblance
between these two objects, but whether there
is a characteristic difference ; and surely
there is a sufficient distinction in all economical investigations between a free man, and
the horse, the machine, or the food which he
uses, to warrant a different designation, especially when one of the greatest objects of all
economical investigations, and certainly the
most worthy, has been how to secure at all
times a full sufficiency of the produce of industry extrinsic to man as compared with man
himself.

It has been hitherto usual to say, that the
happiness of the labouring classes of society
depends chiefly upon the rate at which the
capital of the country increases, compared
with its population ; but if the capital of the
country includes its population, there is no
meaning in the statement. Yet hardly any
writer that I know of has more frequently

made this statement than Mr. Macculloch himself. Nothing, indeed, can show more strikingly the extreme difficulty of maintaining consistently new and unusual definitions, than the frequency with which he seems to be compelled to use terms in their old and accustomed sense, notwithstanding the different definitions which he has given of them.

Thus, in his very peculiar and most untenable argument on the effects of absenteeism in Ireland, one of the reasons which he gives, why the absence of the landlords does not diminish the wealth of that country is, that they do not remove any *capital* from it, but merely what they would spend on their own gratifications. If, however, the definition of the capital of a country, as stated by Mr. Macculloch, be "*that portion of the produce of industry existing in it* which can be made directly available either to the support of human existence or to the facilitating of production," it follows necessarily that they remove a considerable quantity of capital, as it will hardly be denied that the corn, cattle, and butter produced from their estates (which, after all the mystery about bills of exchange is done away, are practically the main articles exported to England for the payment of their rents) may be made directly available to the support of human existence.

Mr. Macculloch is also disposed to recommend emigration as one of the best means of relieving the distress of Ireland, by altering the proportion between capital and labour ; but if, according to him, in all economical discussions, man is to be considered as capital, precisely like the machine which he uses or the food which he consumes, the emigration of a portion of the population will be to deprive the country of a portion of its capital, which has always been considered as most pernicious. Whatever, therefore, may be the merits or demerits of Mr. Macculloch's reasoning on these subjects, independently of his definitions, it is obvious that the application of his definitions at once destroys it.

It need hardly be repeated, that in all the less strict sciences, definitions and classifications are seldom perfect and complete ; but no reasonable man will refuse to take advantage of an imperfect instrument which is essentially useful, if no other more perfect one can be obtained. If it be found useful, with a view to an explanation of the causes of the wealth of nations, to make a distinction between the labours of agriculturists and manufactures, as compared with menial servants, followers, and buffoons, the utility of this distinction is not destroyed, though its perfect accuracy may be impeached, because, in a few instances, the labour of the menial servant is 'very similar to that of the productive labourer. The classification is formed upon the general character and general effects of one sort of industry as compared with another; and if, in these respects, the line of distinction is sufficiently marked, it is mere useless cavilling to dwell upon particular instances.*

* This is very justly stated in Mr. Mill's "Elements of Political Economy," ch. iv. sec. i. p. 219, 2d edit. : both Mr. Ricardo and Mr. Mill, indeed, fully allow the distinction between productive and unproductive labour. M. Say, though he calls the labour of the menial servant productive, makes a distinction between the labour which is productive of *material* products and the labour

But even in the very case on which Mr.
Macculloch lays his principal stress, the difference is such as fully to warrant a different
classification. It is, no doubt, true that, to
have a fire in an attic in London, it is equally
necessary that the coals should be brought
up stairs from the cellar, as that they should
be brought up from the bottom of the coal-
mine to the surface : it is equally true that
there is some resemblance between carrying
coals from the bottom of a house to the top,
and carrying them from the bottom of a mine
to the top ; but there is still a most decided
and characteristic difference in the two cases.

The miner is paid by the owner or worker
of the mine, for the express purpose of in-

which is productive of *immaterial* products. Of the
latter products he says, " En favorisant leur multiplication, on ne fait rien pour la richesse, on ne fait que
pour la consommation."—*Table Analytique*, liv. i. ch.
13. This is a most characteristic difference ; and
though I prefer the classification of Adam Smith, as
more simple, I should allow that, on these principles,
the causes of the wealth of nations may be clearly explained. But I own myself utterly at a loss to conceive
how they can be explained, if all labour be considered
as equally productive.

creasing his wealth ; the value of the miner's labour is, therefore, charged with a profit upon the price of the coals ; and the result of it would regularly enter into any estimate of national wealth. But when the same owner or worker of coal-mines pays a menial servant for bringing coals up from the yard to the drawing-room, he pays him for the express purpose of facilitating and rendering more convenient and agreeable, the consumption of that wealth which he had obtained through the instrumentality of the miner. The two instruments are used for purposes distinctly different, one to assist in obtaining wealth, the other to assist in consuming it. In an inquiry into the causes of the wealth of nations, I cannot easily conceive a more distinct and useful line of demarcation.

On the same principle, if it be found useful with a view to explanations, to distinguish, by a different name, the stock destined for immediate consumption, from the stock employed or kept, with a view to profit, surely we must not wait to investigate the peculiar talents of each individual, before we venture

to characterise the nature of his expenditure;
and if we find such men as Arkwright and
Watt * most naturally and properly reserving,
for their immediate consumption, the means
of keeping up a handsome or splendid esta-
blishment for the gratification of themselves,
their family, and their friends, make an exception in their favour, and call such an expenditure an outlay of capital, instead of a
consumption of revenue, as we should call it
in the case of all ordinary persons. Such an
inquiry would impose a duty upon the writers
in political economy, which it would be perfectly absurd to attempt to fulfil, as it would
quite defeat the end of the proposed classifications; and with regard to the distinguished
characters adverted to, it would surely be
most unnecessary. In an estimate of national
wealth, the genius of a Newton or a Milton
is necessarily underrated, which only shows
that there are other sources of admiration
and delight besides wealth. But such men
as Arkwright and Watt are quite safe in the
hands of the political economist. The re-

* Elem. of Polit. Econ. part ii. p. 93.

sult of their genius and labour is exactly of
that description which is estimated in the
very great addition which it makes to the
capital and revenue of the country, in the
most natural and ordinary acceptation of these
terms. And when the effects of their genius
have been estimated in this way, it would not
only lead to inextricable difficulty, but it
would be obviously a double entry, to estimate, in addition, the value of the men as extraordinary machines. It would be like estimating the value of a commodity produced
by a skilful artificer, and then adding his high
wages, and putting both into an estimate of
national wealth.

But it is difficult to say what may not be
called wealth, or what labour may not be
called productive, in Mr. Macculloch's nomenclature. According to his view of the subject,
any sort of exertion, or any sort of consumption
which tends, however *indirectly*, to encourage
production, ought to be denominated productive; and before we venture to call the most
trivial sort of exercise or amusement, such as
blowing bubbles, or building houses of cards

unproductive, we must wait to see whether
the person so employed does not work the
harder for it afterwards.* But, not to
mention the impossibility of any, the most
useful classification, if such doctrines were
admitted, and we were required to wait
the result in each particular case, and make
exceptions accordingly, I will venture to
affirm, that if we once break down the distinction between the labour which is so
directly productive of wealth as to be estimated in the value of the object produced,
and the labour or exertion, which is so indirectly a cause of wealth, that its effect is incapable of definite estimation, we must necessarily introduce the greatest confusion into the
science of political economy, and render the
causes of the wealth of nations inexplicable.
There is no kind of exertion or amusement
which may not, upon this principle, be called
productive. Walking, riding, driving, card-
playing, billiard-playing, &c. &c. may all be,
indirectly, causes of production ; and according to Mr. Macculloch, "it is very like a tru-

* Princip. of Polit. Econ., part iv. p. 409.

ism, to say, that what is a cause of production must be productive."*

But of all the indirect causes of production, the most powerful, beyond all question, is consumption.

If man were not to consume, how scanty, comparatively, would be the produce of the earth. Consumption, therefore, is the main fundamental cause of production ; and if we are to put indirect causation on a footing with direct causation, as suggested by Mr. Macculloch, we must rank in the same class, the manufacturer and the billiard player, the producer and the consumer.

It is impossible that the science of political economy should not most essentially suffer from such a confusion of terms. Nothing can be clearer, than that, with a view to any thing like precision, and the means of intelligible explanation, it is absolutely necessary to designate by a different name the labour which is directly productive of wealth, from that which merely encourages it.

Another most extraordinary and inconceiv-

* Princip, of Polit. Econ., part iv. p. 411.

able misnomer of Mr. Macculloch is, the extension of the term labour to all the operations of nature, and every variety of profits.

Adam Smith, and all other writers, who
have happened to fall in my way, have meant,
by the term labour, when unaccompanied by
any specific adjunct, the exertions of human
beings ; and by the term wages of labour,
the remuneration, whether in produce or money, paid to those human beings for their
exertions. When Mr. Ricardo stated, that
commodities exchanged with each other according to the quantity of labour worked up
in them, there cannot be the least doubt that
he meant the quantity of human labour immediately employed in their production, together
with that portion of human labour worked up
in the fixed and circulating capitals consumed
in aiding such production. And it is un-
doubtedly true, referring merely to the relation of one commodity to another, and supposing all other things the same ; that is,
supposing profits to be the same, the proportion of fixed and circulating capitals to be the
same, and the duration of the fixed capitals

and the times of the returns of the circulating
capitals the same, that then the relative values
of the commodities will be determined by the
quantity of human labour worked up in each.

But Mr. Macculloch could not but see that
it was scarcely possible to take up two commodities, of different kinds, in which all these
things would be the same, and, consequently,
that such a supposition would be so inapplicable to the mass of commodities, as to be
perfectly useless ; and yet, without such a
supposition, the proposition would be obviously false.

Instead, however, of correcting Mr. Ricardo's proposition, as he was naturally called
upon to do, by adding to the human labour
worked up in the commodity, any other element which was found ordinarily to affect its
value, and calling it by its ordinary name, he
chose to retain Mr. Ricardo's language, but
entirely to alter its meaning. There is nothing that may not be proved by a new definition. A composition of flour, milk, suet,
and stones in a plum-pudding ; if by stones
be meant plums. Upon this principle, Mr.

Macculloch undertakes to show, that commodities do really exchange with each other according to the quantity of labour employed upon them; and it must be acknowledged, that in the instances which he has chosen he has not been deterred by apparent difficulties. He has taken the bull by the horns. The cases are nearly as strong as that of the plum-pudding.*

They are the two following—namely, that the increase of value which a cask of wine acquires, by being kept a certain number of years untouched in a cellar, is occasioned by the increased quantity of labour employed upon it; and that an oak tree of a hundred years' growth, worth 25*l*., which may not have been touched by man, beast, or machine for a century, derives its whole value from labour.

Mr. Macculloch acknowledges that Mr. Ricardo was inclined to modify his grand principle, that the exchangeable value of commodities depended on the quantity of labour required for their production, so far as to allow that the additional exchangeable value that

* Principles of Polit. Econ., part iii., pp. 313, 317.

is sometimes given to commodities, by keeping them after they have been purchased or produced until they become fit to be used, was not to be considered as an effect of labour, but as an equivalent for the profits which the capital laid out on the commodities would have yielded had it been actually employed.* This was looking at the subject in the true point of view, and showing that he would not get out of the difficulty by changing the meaning of the term labour ; but Mr. Macculloch says—

" I confess, however, notwithstanding the hesitation I cannot but feel in differing from so great an authority, that I see no good reason for making this exception. Suppose, to illustrate the principle, that a cask of new wine, which cost 50*l.*, is put into a cellar, and that at the end of twelve months it is worth 55*l.*, the question is, whether ought the 5*l.* of additional value given to the wine to be considered as a compensation for the time the 50*l.* worth of capital has been locked up, or ought it to be considered as the value of

* Principles of Polit. Econ., part iii. p. 313.

additional labour actually laid out on the wine. I think that it ought to be considered in the latter point of view, and for this, as it appears to me a most satisfactory and conclusive reason, that if we keep a commodity, as a cask of wine which has not arrived at maturity, and on which therefore *a change or effect is to be produced,* it will be possessed of additional value at the year's end ; whereas, had we kept a cask of wine which had *already arrived at maturity,* and on which no beneficial or desirable effect could be produced for a hundred or a thousand years, it would not have been worth a single additional farthing. This seems to prove incontrovertibly that the additional value acquired by the wine during the period it has been kept in the cellar is not a compensation or return for time, but for the effect or change that has been produced on it. Time cannot of itself produce any effect, it merely affords space for really efficient causes to operate ; and it is therefore clear, that it can have nothing to do with the value."*

* Principles of Polit. Econ., part iii. p. 313.

On this passage it should be remarked, in the first place, that the question stated in it is not the main question in reference to the new meaning which Mr. Macculloch must give to the term labour, in order to make out his proposition. He acknowledges that the increased value acquired by the wine is either owing to the operation of nature during the year in improving its quality, or to the profits acquired by the capitalist for being deprived for a year from using his capital of 50*l.* in any other way. But in either case Mr. Macculloch's language is quite unwarranted. When he uses the expression, " *additional labour actually laid out upon the wine,*" who could possibly imagine that, instead of meaning human labour, he meant the processes carried on by nature in a cask of wine during the time that it is kept. This is at once giving an entirely new meaning to the term labour.

But, further, it is most justly stated by Mr. Ricardo, that when the powers of nature can be called into action in unlimited abundance, she always works *gratis ;* and her processes never add to the value, though they may add very greatly to the utility of the objects to which they are applied.

This truth is also fully adopted and strongly stated by Mr. Macculloch himself. " All the rude products (he says) and all the productive powers and capacities of nature are gratuitously offered to man. Nature is not niggardly or parsimonious ; she neither demands nor receives an equivalent for her favours. An object which it does not require any portion of labour to appropriate or to adapt to our use may be of the very highest utility, but as it is the free gift of nature, it is utterly impossible it can be possessed of the smallest value."* Consequently, as the processes which are carrying on in the cask of wine, while it is kept, are unquestionably the free gift of nature, and are at the service of all who want them, it is utterly impossible, even if their effects were ten times greater than they are, that they should add in the smallest degree to the price of the wine. It is, no doubt, perfectly true, as stated by Mr. Macculloch, that if wine were not im-

* Principles of Polit. Econ., part ii. p. 69.

proved by keeping, it would not be worth a
single additional farthing after being kept a
hundred or even a thousand years. But this
proves nothing but that, in that case, no one
would ever think of keeping wine longer than
was absolutely necessary for its convenient
sale or convenient consumption.

The improvement which wine derives from
keeping is unquestionably the cause of its
being kept ; but when on this account the
wine-merchant has kept his wine, the additional price which he is enabled to put upon
it is regulated upon principles totally distinct
from the average degree of improvement
which the wine acquires. It is regulated exclusively, as stated by Mr. Ricardo, by the
average profits which the capital engaged in
keeping the wine would have yielded if it had
been actively employed ; and that this is the
regulating principle of the additional price,
and not the degree of improvement, is quite
certain : because it would be universally allowed that if, in the case supposed by Mr.
Macculloch, the ordinary rate of profits had
been 20 per cent., instead of 10 per cent., a

cask of new wine, worth 50*l.*, after it had been kept a year, would have been increased in value 10*l.* instead of 5*l.*, although the processes of nature and the improvement of the wine were precisely the same in the two cases; and there cannot be the least doubt, as I said before, that if the quality of wine, by a year's keeping, were ordinarily improved in a degree ten times as great as at present, the prices of wines would not be raised; because, if they were so raised, all wine-merchants who sold kept wines would be making greater profits than other dealers.

Nothing then can be clearer than that the additional value of the kept wine is derived from the additional amount of profits of which it is composed, determined by the time for which the capital was advanced and the ordinary rate of profits.

The value of the oak tree of a hundred years' growth is derived, in a very considerable degree, from the same cause; though, in rich and cultivated countries, where alone it could be worth 25*l.*, rent would necessarily form a part of this value.

If the number of acorns necessary on an average to rear one good oak were planted by the hand of man, they would be planted on appropriated land ; and as land is limited in quantity, the powers of vegetation in the land cannot be called into action by every one who is in possession of acorns, in the same way as the improving operations of nature may be called into action by every person who possesses a cask of wine. But setting this part of the value aside, and supposing the acorns to be planted at a certain expense, it is quite clear, that almost the whole of the remaining value would be derived from the compound interest or profits upon the advances of the labour required for the first planting of the acorns, and the subsequent protection of the young trees. A much larger part, therefore, of the final value of the tree than of the final value of the wine would be owing to profits.

Now, if we were to compare an oak tree, worth 25*l*., with a quantity of hardware worth the same sum, the value of which was chiefly made up of human labour ; and as the reason

why these two objects were of the same value,
were to state that the same quantity of labour
had been worked up in them—we should obviously state a direct falsity, according to the
common usage of language ; and nothing
could make the statement true, but the magi-
cal influence of a new meaning given to the
term labour. But to make labour mean profits, or fermentation, or vegetation, or rent,
appears to me quite as unwarrantable as to
make stones mean plums.

To *measure* profits by labour is totally a
different thing. Adam Smith always keeps
wages, profits, and rent quite distinct ; and
when he mentions one of them, never thinks
of including in the same term any other. But
he observes, that " labour *measures* the value
not only of that part of the price of a commo-
modity which resolves itself into labour, but
of that which resolves itself into rent, and of
that which resolves itself into profit."* This
is perfectly just ; and, in particular, nothing
can be more natural and obvious than to measure by labour the increase of value which
commodities derive from profits ; because

* Wealth of Nations, b. i. c. vi.

profits are a per centage upon the advances, and the main original advances in the great mass of commodities are the necessary quantity of labour.*

Thus, if a hundred days' labour be advanced for a year,* in order to produce a commodity, and the rate of profits be 10 per cent., it is impossible in any way to represent so correctly the increase of value which the commodity derives from profits as by adding 10 per cent., or whatever may be the rate of profits, to the quantity of labour actually employed, and saying, that the completed commodity when sold would be worth ten days' labour more than the quantity of labour worked up in it. On the other hand, if we were ignorant of the rate of profits, but found that a hundred days' labour advanced for a year would produce a commodity which would ordinarily sell for the value of one hundred and ten days, we might safely conclude that ordinary profits were 10 per cent.

* It must always be recollected, that the advance of a certain number of days' labour necessarily involves the wages paid for them, however these wages may vary in quantity. But the essential advance is the quantity of labour, not the quantity of money or corn.

Now, if we were to compare two commodities, on each of which a hundred days' labour had been employed, and one of them could be brought to market immediately, the other in not less time than a year, it is quite obvious, that we could not say that they would exchange with each other according to the quantity of labour worked up in them ; but we evidently could say, that they would exchange with each other according to the quantity of labour *and of profits* worked up in them, and that one of them would be 10 per cent. more valuable than the other, because profits had added the value of ten days' labour to the labour actually employed upon the one ; while there being no profits in the other, its value was only in proportion to the labour actually employed upon it.

And in general, while the slightest examination of what is passing around us must convince us that commodities, under deduction of rent and taxes, *do not* ordinarily exchange with each according to the quantity of human labour worked up in them, the same examination will convince us that, under

the same deduction, they *do* ordinarily exchange with each other, according to the
quantity of human labour *and of profits* worked
up in them ; and further, that the quantity
of human labour worked up in them, with the
profits upon the advances for the time that
they have been advanced, is correctly measured by the quantity of human labour of the
same kind which the commodity so composed
will ordinarily command.

We must carefully, therefore, distinguish
between *measuring* profits by labour, and
meaning profits by labour ; and while the first
is obviously justifiable, and may be in the
highest degree useful, it must be allowed,
that the latter contradicts all the most obvious rules for the use of terms : it contradicts the usage of common conversation: it
contradicts the highest authorities in the
science of political economy : it embarrasses
all explanations ; and it cannot be maintained
with consistency.

Though Mr. Macculloch's work affords
other instances of a want of attention, on a
point so important in all philosophical dis-

cussions, as appropriate and consistent definitions, I will only notice further, his use of the term *real*. He applies it to wages, in two senses entirely different.

In part iii. p. 294, he says, "But if the variation in the rate of wages be *real*, and not nominal, that is, if the labourer be getting either a greater or less *proportion of the produce of his industry*, or a greater or less quantity of money of invariable value, this will not happen." Here, it is evident that Mr. Macculloch applies the term *real* to wages, in the sense of proportional wages, that is, as Mr. Ricardo applied it.

In part iii. p. 365, Mr. Macculloch says, "If the productiveness of industry were to diminish, proportional wages might rise, notwithstanding that *real wages*, or the *absolute amount of the produce* of industry falling to the share of the labourer, might be diminished. Here, the term real wages is used as synonymous with the absolute amount of produce falling to the share of the labourer, that is, in the sense in which Adam Smith has applied it.

I have already observed, that Adam Smith's application of the term *real wages*, to the absolute quantity of the produce earned by the labourer, seems to be a most natural one; and Mr. Ricardo's application of the same term to the *proportion* of the produce earned by the labourer, a most unnatural one. Mr. Macculloch, therefore, was quite right, in introducing the term *proportionate wages*, to express Mr. Ricardo's meaning; but why not adhere to it? Why should he, in some places, mean, by real wages, proportionate wages, and, in other places, something totally different.

In the application of the term *real* to value, Mr. Macculloch adopts the meaning of Mr. Ricardo. He says, indeed, " that it is to Mr. Ricardo's sagacity, in distinguishing between the quantity of labour required to produce commodities, and the quantity of labour for which they will exchange, and in showing, that while the first is undeniably correct as a measure of their real, and generally speaking, of their exchangeable values, the second, instead of being an equivalent proposition, is requently opposed to the first, and consequently, quite inaccurate, that the science is indebted for one of its greatest improvements."*

I should be sorry to think that Mr. Ricardo's services to the science of political economy should rest principally upon the frail foundation, on which they are here placed; a foundation, which, as we have seen, Mr. Macculloch himself cannot defend, without totally altering the meaning of Mr. Ricardo's words.

This is evident, in various passages of Mr. Macculloch's work. In his section on value, part ii. p. 216, he thus expresses himself: "assuming the *toil and trouble of acquiring any thing* to be the measure of its

* Principles of Polit. Econ., part iii. p. 223. This is a most remarkable passage to come from Mr. Macculloch, who, though he agrees with Mr. Ricardo in words, has, in reality, deserted him, and agrees in substance with Adam Smith. According to the new meaning, which Mr. Macculloch has given to the term profits—the quantity of labour required to produce a commodity, is precisely equal to the quantity of labour for which it will ordinarily exchange, and certainly not equal to what Mr. Ricardo meant by the quantity of labour bestowed upon it.

real value, or of the *esteem* in which it is
held by its possessor." Again, he says,
p. 219, "the real value of a commodity, or
*the estimation in which it is held by its pos-
sessor*, is measured or determined by the
quantity of labour required to produce or obtain it."

In these two passages, he obviously iden-
tifies the real value of a commodity with
the estimation in which it is held. But,
surely, in this case, the term real must be
applied as Adam Smith applies it, and not
as Mr. Ricardo applies it? Can it be con-
tended for a moment, that a commodity,
which, on account of the necessary remuneration for profits, sells for ten per cent. above
the value of the human labour worked up in
it, is not held in *higher estimation*, than a
commodity which sells for ten per cent. less,
on account of the value of the labour employed upon it not having been increased by
profits? Would it not be absolutely certain,
that if the latter could be obtained by the
sacrifice of a hundred days' labour, it would
be necessary to make the sacrifice of a hundred

and ten days' labour, or some equivalent for
it, in order to obtain the former? Consequently it follows necessarily, that if the real
value of a commodity be considered as synonymous with the estimation in which it is
held, such value must be measured by the
quantity of labour which it will command,
and not the quantity worked up in it.

Mr. Macculloch thus states Mr. Ricardo's
main proposition :* " a commodity, produced
by a certain quantity of labour, will, in the
state of the market now supposed, (that is,
when the market is not affected by either real
or artificial monopolies, and when the supply
of commodities is equal to the effectual demand,) uniformly exchange for, or buy any
other commodity, produced by the same
quantity of labour."

Now, if the term labour be taken in the
sense in which it is used by Mr. Ricardo, the
proposition is contradicted by universal experience. If, on the other hand, the term
labour be considered as including profits, the
proposition is true; but only because it is

* Principles of Polit. Econ., part iii. s. 1. p. 221.

a totally different one from that of Mr. Ricardo, owing to a most unwarrantable perversion of terms.

It appears, then, on the whole, that although Mr. Macculloch has at different times compared Adam Smith to Newton and to Locke, he has, in the definition and application of his terms, differed from him on almost all the most important subjects of Political Economy,—in the definition of wealth, the definition of capital, the definition of productive and unproductive labour, the definition of profits, the definition of labour simply, and the definition of *real value*, though, in the last instance, it is rather professedly than substantially.*

However highly I may respect the authority of Adam Smith, and however inconvenient at first a great change of terms and meanings must necessarily be, yet if it could

* A person who uses a term in a particular sense practically defines it in that sense. Mr. Macculloch sometimes makes what have hitherto always been considered as profits mean labour ; and sometimes makes labour, when used simply without any adjunct, mean fermentation, vegetation, or profits.

be made out that such changes would essentially facilitate the explanation and improve
ment of the science of political economy, 1
should have been the last to oppose them.
But after considering them with much attention, I own I feel the strongest conviction that
they are eminently the reverse of being *useful*,
with a view to an explanation of the *nature*
and causes of the wealth of nations ; or, in
more modern, though not more appropriate
phrase, the *production, distribution, and con-*
sumption of wealth.

I have too much respect for Mr. Macculloch to
suppose that he has differed from Adam Smith
on so many points with the intention of giving
to his work a greater air of originality. This
is, no doubt, a feeling which not unfrequently
operates in favour of changes ; but I do not
think it did on the present occasion. I should
rather suppose that he adopted them in consequence of seeing some objections to Adam
Smith's definitions, without being sufficiently
aware that, in the less stric sciences, nothing
is so easy as to find some objection to a defi-

nition, and nothing so difficult as to substitute an unobjectionable one in its place.

Whether the definitions substituted for those of Adam Smith on the present occasion have removed the objections to them which Mr. Macculloch may have felt, I cannot be a competent judge ; but even supposing them to have done this, I think I can confidently affirm that they have left other objections, beyond all comparison greater and more embarrassing. And on this point I would beg those of my readers who are inclined to pay attention to these subjects, seriously and candidly to trace the consequences to the science of political economy, in regard to its explanation and practical application, of adopting Mr. Macculloch's definitions. They are not, indeed, all his own ; but the very extraordinary extension which he has given to the term capital, the making of no distinction between directly productive consumption and consumption that is only indirectly productive ; and the extension of the term labour, without any adjunct, to mean profits, fermentation, and vegetation, belong, I believe, exclusively to Mr. Macculloch ; and, I think, it will be found that they are beyond the rest strikingly calculated to introduce uncertainty and confusion into the science.

The tendency of some of our most popular writers to innovate without improving, and their marked inattention to facts, leading necessarily to differences of opinion and uncertainty of conclusion, have been the main causes which have of late thrown some discredit on the science of political economy Nor can this be a matter of much surprise though it may be of regret.

At a period, when all the merchants of our own country, and many in others, find the utmost difficulty in employing their capitals so as to obtain ordinary profits, they are repeatedly told that, according to the principles of political economy, no difficulty can ever be found in employing capital, if it be laid out in the production of the proper articles ; and that any distress which they may have suffered is exclusively owing to a wrong application of their capital, such as " the production of cottons, which were not wanted, instead of broad cloths, which were wanted."* They are, further, gravely assured, that if they find any difficulty in exchanging what they have produced, for what they wish to obtain for it, " they have an obvious resource at hand; they can abandon the production of the commodities which they do not want, and apply themselves directly to the production of those that they *do* want, or of substitutes for them;"† and this consolatory recommendation is perhaps addressed to a merchant who is desirous of obtaining, by the employment of his capital at the ordinary rate of profits, such an income as will enable him to get a governess for his daughters, and to send his boys to school and college.

At such times, assertions like these, and the proposal of such a remedy, appear to me little different from an assertion, on supposed philosophical principles, that it *cannot* rain, when crowds of people are getting wet

* Macculloch's Principles of Polit. Econ., part ii. p. 189.
† Id. p. 190.

through, and the proposal to go without
clothes in order to prevent the inconvenience
arising from a wet coat. If assertions so
contrary to the most glaring facts, and reme-
dies so preposterously ridiculous, in a civilized
country,* are said to be dictated by the principles of political economy, it cannot be
matter of wonder that many have little faith
in them. And till the theories of popular
writers on political economy cease to be in

* I own I want words to express the astonishment
I feel at the proposal of such a remedy. A man, under
the intoxication of what he conceives to be a new and
important discovery, may be excused for occasionally
making a rash statement ; but that a proposal directly
involving the discontinuance of the division of labour
should, in a civilized country, be repeated over and
over again by succeeding writers, and considered as an
obvious resource in a sudden fall of profits, absolutely
passes my comprehension. What a strange and most
inapt illustration too, is it to talk about the possessors
of broad cloths wanting to change them for silks !
Who ever heard of a great producer of any commodity
wishing to obtain an equivalent for it in some *one* other
sort of completed commodity ? If he is to produce
what he wants, it must not be silks, but raw materials,
tools, corn, meat, coats, hats, shoes and stockings, &c.
&c. ; and this is the *obvious resource* which is at hand in
a glut ! ! !

direct opposition to general experience ; and till some steadiness is given to the science by a greater degree of care among its professors, not to alter without improving,—it cannot be expected that it should attain that general influence in society which (its principles being just) would be of the highest practical utility.

Chapter VIII.

ON THE DEFINITION AND USE OF TERMS BY THE AUTHOR OF " A CRITICAL DISSERTATION ON THE NATURE, MEASURE, AND CAUSES OF VALUE."

IT might be thought that I was not called upon to notice the deviations from the most obvious rules for the use of terms in a *Critical Dissertation on the Nature, Measure, and Causes of Value*, by an anonymous writer. But the great importance of the subject itself at the present moment, when it may be said to be *sub judice*, the tone of scientific precision in which the dissertation is written, notwithstanding its fundamental errors, and the impression which it is understood to have made among some considerable political economists, seem to call for and justify attention to it.

The author, in his preface, observes, that " Writers on political economy have generally contented themselves with a short definition of the term value, and a distinction of the property denoted by it into several kinds, and have then proceeded to employ the word with various degrees of laxity. Not one of them has brought into distinct view the nature of the idea represented by this term, or the inferences which a full perception of its meaning immediately suggests ; and the neglect of this preliminary has created differences of opinion and perplexities of thought which otherwise could never have existed."*

Now it appears to me, that the author, at his first setting out, has in an eminent degree fallen into the very errors which he has here animadverted upon.

He begins by stating, very justly, that " value, in its ultimate sense, appears to mean the esteem in which any object is held ;" and then proceeds to state, in the most lax and inconsequent manner, that " It is only when objects are considered together as subjects of preference or exchange that the specific feeling of value can arise. When they are so considered, our esteem for one

* Preface, p. 5.

object, or our wish to possess it, may be equal
to, or greater, or less than our esteem for
another ; *it may, for instance, be doubly as
great*, or, in other words, we would give one
of the former for two of the latter. So long
as we regarded objects singly, we might feel
a great degree of admiration or fondness for
them, but we could not express our emotions
in any definite manner. When, however,
we regard two objects, as subjects of choice
or exchange, we appear to acquire the power
of expressing our feelings with precision ; we
say, for instance, that one a is, in our estimation, equal to two b. . . . The value of a is
expressed by the quantity b, for which it will
exchange, and the value of b is, in the same
way, expressed by the quantity of a."*

So, then, it appears, as a consequence of
value, meaning the esteem in which an object
is held, that if there were two sorts of fruit
in a country, called a and b, both very plentiful in the summer, and both very scarce in
the winter ; and if in both seasons they were
to bear the same relation to each other, the

* Dissertation on Value, c. 1. p. 3.

feelings of the inhabitants with regard to the fruit *a* would be *expressed with precision*, by saying that, as it would always command the same quantity of the fruit *b*, it would continue to be of the same value—that is, would be held in the same estimation in summer as in winter.

It appears, further, that in a country where there were only deer, and no beavers or other products to compare them with, the specific feeling of value for deer could not arise among the inhabitants ; although, on account of the high esteem in which they were held, any man would willingly walk fifty miles in order to get one ! ! These are, to be sure, very strange conclusions, but they follow directly from the presvious statements.

The author, however, nothing daunted, goes on to say, that " If from any consideration, or number of considerations, men esteem one *a* as highly as two *b*, and are willing to exchange the two commodities in that ratio, it may be correctly said that *a* has the power of commanding two *b*, or that *b* has the power of commanding half of *a*."

" The definition of Adam Smith, therefore, that the value of an object expresses the power of purchasing other goods which the possession of that object conveys, is substantially correct ; and as it is plain and intelligible, it may be taken as the basis of our subsequent reasonings without any further metaphysical investigation."*

In a Critical Dissertation on Value, which is introduced with a heavy complaint against all preceding political economists for neglecting the preliminary labour necessary to give a full perception of its meaning, it might naturally have been expected, that previous to the final adoption of the meaning in which it was intended to use the term throughout the dissertation, the consideration, or number of considerations, which induce men to prefer one object to another, or to give two *b* for one *a*, should be carefully investigated. But nothing of this kind is done. A definition of the value of an object by Adam Smith, which, as he afterwards clearly shows, requires explanation and modification, is arbitrarily

---

* Dissertation on Value, c. 1. p. 4.

adopted, or, in the language of the author, is " taken as the basis of his subsequent reasonings, without any further metaphysical investigation."

That this first general description of value in exchange by Adam Smith does not, without further explanation, convey to the reader the prevailing meaning which he himself attaches to the term, is obvious in many passages of his work, and particularly in his elaborate inquiry into the value of silver during the four last centuries. He there shows, in the most satisfactory manner, that, in the progress of cultivation and improvement, there is a class of commodities, such as cattle, wood, pigs, poultry, &c., which, on account of their becoming comparatively more scarce and difficult of attainment, necessarily rise in value; yet he particularly states, that this rise in their value is not connected with any degradation in the value of silver,* although it is obvious that, other things being the same, a pound of silver would have a smaller power of purchasing other goods.

* Wealth of Nations, b. i. c. xi.

Nothing, indeed, can be clearer than that
this general description of value requires further explanation. There is the greatest difference imaginable between an increased
power in any object of purchasing other goods,
arising from its scarcity and the increased
difficulty of procuring it ; and the increase
of its power to purchase other goods arising
from the increased plenty of such goods and
the increased facility of procuring them. Nor
is it easy to conceive any distinction more
vital to the subject of *value*, as the term is
generally understood, or more necessary to
" a full perception of its meaning."

I cannot but think, therefore, that the author, under all the circumstances of the case,
was not justified in adopting this definition of
Adam Smith without further investigation.

But the adoption of this definition by the
author in so unceremonious a manner, though
quite inconsistent with the declarations in the
preface, and most unpromising in regard to
any improvement of the science which might
have been expected from the dissertation, is

by no means the gravest offence which he has committed in the opening of his subject.

Adam Smith's definition, taken as it stands, however imperfect it may be, would still serve as a rough but useful standard of value in those cases where, in using the most ordinary forms of expression, some kind of standard is tacitly referred to, and no other more accurate one had been adopted.

But how is this definition of Adam Smith to be interpreted? If we understand it in the sense usually conveyed by the terms employed, it is impossible to doubt that by the power of purchasing other goods is meant the power of purchasing other goods generally. Who, then, could have conceived before-hand that the author would have inferred from this definition that he was justified in representing the power of purchasing other goods by the power of purchasing any one sort of goods which might first come to hand?—so that, considering the value of money in this country to be proportioned to its general power of purchasing, it would be correct to say that

the value of an ounce of silver was proportioned to the quantity of apples which it would
command; and that when it commanded more
apples, the value of silver rose—when it commanded fewer apples, the value of silver fell.

It is, no doubt, quite allowable to compare
any two commodities whatever together in
regard to their value in exchange, and,
among others, silver and apples. It is also
allowable to say, though it would in general
sound very strange, that the value of an ounce
of silver, *estimated in apples*, is the quantity
of apples it will command, provided that, by
thus using the qualifying expression *estimated
in apples*, immediately after the word value,
we distinctly give notice to the reader that we
are not going to speak of the exchangeable
value of silver generally, according to the
definition of Adam Smith, but merely in the
very confined sense of its relation to one particular article. But if, without this distinct
notice to the reader, we simply say that the
value of an ounce of silver is expressed by
the quantity of apples for which it will ex-

change, or, in the words of the author, that " the value of a is expressed by the quantity of b, for which it will exchange," nothing can be more clear than that we use the term value in a manner totally unwarranted by the previous definition, that is, in a sense quite distinct from that in which Adam Smith uses it in the description of value adopted by the author.

Putting the corn and the circulating medium of a country out of the question, the relations of which to labour and the costs of producing various commodities are tolerably well known, I think no one, in ordinary conversation, has ever been heard to express the general power of purchasing by the power of purchasing some one particular commodity. I certainly, at least, myself never recollect to have heard these two very distinct meanings confounded. It would, indeed, sound very strange, if a person returning from India, on being asked what was the value of money in that country, were to mention the quantity of English broad cloth which a given quantity of money would exchange for, and to infer, in consequence, that the value of money was lower in India than in England.

In regard to the opinions and practice of other writers on political economy, most of them have considered the general power of purchasing, and the power of purchasing a particular commodity as so essentially distinct, that they have given them different names. The only authority quoted with approbation by the author, is Colonel Torrens, whose views, as to the nature of value, appear to him, he says, to be sounder than those of any other writer. Yet, what does Colonel Torrens say on this subject?— "The term exchangeable value expresses the power of purchasing with respect to commodities in general. The term price denotes the same power with respect to some particular commodity, the quantity of which is given. Thus, when I speak of the *exchangeable value* of cotton as rising or falling, I imply, that it will purchase a greater or less quantity of corn, and wine, and labour, and other marketable commodities; but when I talk of the *price* of cotton as rising or falling, I mean, that it will purchase a greater or less quantity of some one particular commodity, such as corn, or wine, or labour, or money, which is either expressed or understood. Exchangeable value may rise, while price falls, or fall while price rises. For example; if cotton were, from any cause, to acquire twice its former power of purchasing, with respect to goods in general, while gold, the particular commodity in which the price of cotton is expressed, rose in a still higher ratio, and acquired four times its former power in the market, then, though the exchangeable value of cotton would be doubled, its price would fall one half. Again; if cotton would purchase only half the former quantity of commodities, while it purchased twice the quantity of some particular commodity, such as corn, or wine, or labour, or money, then its exchangeable value would have sunk one half, while its price, as expressed in corn, or wine, or labour, or money, became double. And again; if cotton, and the particular commodity in which price is expressed, should rise or fall in the same proportion with each other, then the exchangeable value of cotton, or its general power of purchasing, would fluctuate, while its price remained stationary."*

It appears then, that, whether Colonel Torrens's view of value be quite correct or not, he draws the most marked line of distinction possible between the power of purchasing generally, and the power of purchasing a particular commodity, and is decidedly of opinion, that the latter, which is the sense in which the author uses the term value, should not be called value, but price. The authority of Colonel Torrens, therefore, whose views on the subject of value the author considers as so sound, is directly against him.

But not only does Colonel Torrens attach a very different meaning to the term value, from that in which it is used by the author throughout the greatest part of his work, but the author himself, in his notes and illustrations,† has given extracts from almost all the distinguished writers in political economy,

* Production of Wealth, c. i. p. 49.
† p. 242.

expressly for the purpose of showing the universality of an opinion respecting the nature and measure of value directly opposed to his own. The writers to whom he refers, are Adam Smith, Sir James Stuart, Lord Lauderdale, M. Storch, M. Say, Mr. Ricardo, myself, Colonel Torrens, Mrs. Marcet, Mr. Mill, the Templar's Dialogues, and Mr. Blake.

In the case of a proposition the nature of which admits of a logical proof, authority is of no consequence ; but in a question which relates to the meaning to be attached to a particular term, it is quite incredible that any person should thus have ventured to disregard it.

Much, however, of inconsistency, of illogical inference, and disregard of authority, might have been forgiven, if the proposed change in the meaning of the term value would introduce a much greater degree of clearness and precision into the language of political economy, and, in that way, be eminently useful to the progress of the science.

But, what would be the consequence of adopting the meaning which the author at-

taches to the term value, and of allowing,
according to his own words, that "the value
of a is expressed by the quantity of b for
which it will exchange, and the value of b is,
in the same way, expressed by the quantity of
a?" * One of these consequences is strikingly
described in the following passage of the
author's chapter on *Real and Nominal Value*
a distinction which he is pleased to call
unmeaning. " The value of a commodity
denoting its relation in exchange to some
other commodity, we may speak of it as
money-value, corn-value, cloth-value, according to the commodity with which it is compared: and hence there are a thousand
different kinds of value, as many kinds of
value as there are commodities in existence,
and all are equally real and equally nominal."†

This is precision with a vengeance. Now,
though I am very far from intending to say
that the writers on political economy have
been sufficiently agreed as to the precise

* Dissertation on Value, c. i. p. 3.
† c. ii. p. 39.

meaning which they attach to the terms *value of a commodity*, when no express reference is made to the object with which it is to be compared, yet, by drawing a marked line of distinction between what has been called the real value of commodities and their nominal value, or, more correctly, between their *value* and their *price*, they have avoided the prodigious confusion which would arise from a commodity having a thousand or ten thousand different values at the same time. Whenever they use the term value of a commodity alone, and speak of its rising or falling, if they do not mean money-price, they refer either to its power of purchasing generally, or to something expressive of its elementary cost of production.

In either case, some general and very important information is communicated; but the value of a commodity, in the sense understood by the author, might be expressed a hundred different ways, without conveying a rational answer to any person who had inquired about it.

Further; the use of the term *value*, in the

sense understood by the author, is entirely su-
perfluous. It has exactly the same meaning as
the term *price*, except that the term price has
this very decided advantage over it, namely,
that when the price of a commodity is mentioned, without an express reference to any
other object in which it is to be estimated,
political economists have universally agreed
to understand it as referring to money. This
is a prodigious advantage in favour of the
term price, and tends greatly to promote both
facility and precision in the language of political economy. When I ask, what is the
price of wheat in Poland? no one has the least
doubt about my meaning, and I should, without
fail, get the kind of answer I intended. But if I
asked, what was the *value* of wheat in Poland?
I might, according to the author, be answered
in a thousand different ways, all equally proper, and yet not one of the answers be of the
kind I wanted. Of course, whether I use the
term value or price, if I always expressly sub-
join the object to which I mean to refer, it will
be quite indifferent to which term I resort.
But it is vain to suppose that the public will

submit to such constant and unnecessary circumlocution. It would quite alter the language of political economy; and the kind of abbreviation which has taken place in application to the term price could not take place in regard to value, according to the doctrines of the author ; because, when the *value* of a commodity is used alone, like the price of a commodity, no one object rather than another is entitled to a preference for the expression of that value. The author says distinctly in a note,* that money-value has no greater claim to the general term *value* than any other kind of value. It is quite clear, therefore, that if the term value is only to be applied in the sense in which it is applied by the author, it would be much better to exclude it at once from the vocabulary of political economy as utterly useless, and only calculated to produce confusion.

It may be further observed, that the sense in which the author proposes to apply the term value, is so different from the sense in which it is understood in ordinary conver-

* Dissertation on Value, c. iii. p. 58.

sation, and among the best writers, that it would be quite impossible to maintain it with consistency. The author himself, however obstinately, at times, he seems to persevere in the peculiar meaning which he has given to the term value, frequently uses it by itself, without reference to any particular article in which he proposes to express it. Even in the titles of some of his chapters he does this; and when in Chapter XI. he discusses *the distinction between value and riches,* and in Chapter XI. *the causes of value,* we are entitled to complain, that he has not acted according to the instructions which he has given to others, and told us, either expressly, or by implication, in what article the value here mentioned is to be expressed.

Again; when he mentions the value of that corn which is produced on lands paying rent, and when he speaks, as he frequently does, of the value of capital,* he does not tell

---

* Dissertation on Value, c. xi. p. 194, 224. In the question between Colonel Torrens and Mr. Mill, " Whether the value of commodities depends upon capital as the final standard," the author decides against Mr. Mill, but surely without reason. Mr. Mill cannot

us in what he means to express the value of
corn, or of capital, although he thinks that
such a reference, either expressed or implied, is always necessary, and particularly
says, "In the preceding pages it has been
shown, that we can express the value of
a commodity only by the quantity of some
other commodity for which it will exchange."*

The meaning, therefore, which he gives to
the term value is such, that he cannot and
does not maintain it consistently himself,
much less can he expect that others should
so maintain it.

It appears, then, that the author has arbitrarily adopted a meaning of the term
value quite unwarranted by the usage of
ordinary conversation, directly opposed to the

be wrong in thinking, that no progress whatever is
made towards tracing the value of a commodity to its
elements, by saying, that its value is determined by the
value of the capital employed to produce it. The question still remains, how is the value of the capital determined? As to what the author says, p. 202, about the
amount of capital, unless this amount be estimated in
money, which quite alters the question, it is entirely inapplicable as a standard.

* c. viii. p. 160.

authority of the best writers on political economy, pre-eminently and conspicuously useless ; and of such a nature that it cannot be
maintained with consistency.

And what does he do with his definition
after so adopting it ?

He applies it to try the truth of a number
of propositions advanced by different writers,
who, according to his own showing, have
used the term in a very different sense.

This, I own, appears to me much the same
kind of proceeding as if a person were to
define a straight line to be something essentially different from a line lying evenly between its two extremes, and then were gravely
to apply it to one proposition after another
of Euclid, and show, as might easily be done,
granting the definition, that the conclusions
of the Grecian geometer were all wrong.

The perseverance with which the author
proceeds gravely to apply his peculiar definition of value to other writers, who have
defined it differently, is truly curious, and must
be allowed to be a great waste of time and
labour. If, as he says he has repeatedly

stated, " to know the value of an article at any period is merely to know its relation in exchange to some other commodity ;" *   and if, as I believe, no previous writer, in referring to the value of an article at any period ever thought or said that it could be expressed by its relation in exchange to any other contemporary commodity indifferently, it might at once be presumed, without further trouble, that almost all former propositions involving the term value would turn out to be either false or futile.   It was quite unnecessary for him, therefore, to go into the detail ; but as he has done so, it may be useful to follow him in some of his conclusions, as it may assist in drawing attention to a subject which lies at the bottom of many of the difficulties in political economy, and has not been sufficiently considered.

One of the first effects of the author's definition is to destroy the distinction between what many writers of great authority have called *real value*, and *nominal value*.   I have already had occasion to observe, that Adam

* c. vi. p. 135.

Smith, by applying the term *real* wages to express the necessaries and conveniencies of life earned by the labourer, had precluded himself from the power of applying it consistently to the *value* of a commodity, in order to express its power of commanding labour; because it is well known that the same quantity of labour will both produce and command, at different times and under different circumstances, a very different quantity of the necessaries and conveniencies of life. But putting aside for the present this acknowledged inconsistency of Adam Smith, and taking real value as distinguished from nominal in the sense in which the writers who have so applied it intended, the author's observations on these writers are not a little extraordinary.

After noticing the doctrines of Adam Smith, Mr. Ricardo, and myself, on the subject of real and nominal value, he says, " After the disquisition on the nature of value in the preceding chapter, the distinction of it in this way must appear to be merely arbitrary and incapable of being turned to any use. What information is conveyed or what advance in

argument is effected, by telling us that value
estimated in one way is real, but in another,
is nominal ?"*   He afterwards goes on to say,
in reference to a passage in the Templar's
Dialogues, " It would not, however, probably
have been written, had the author attended
to the simple fact, that value must always
imply value in something, and unless that
something is indicated, the word conveys no
information.   Now, as the terms nominal and
real do not denote anything in this way, they
convey no precise information, and are liable
to engender continual disputes, because their
meaning is arbitrarily assumed."†

These appear to me, I confess, to be very
extraordinary observations. It must surely
be allowed, that to compare a commodity
either with the mass of other commodities, or
with the elementary costs of production, is
most essentially distinct from comparing it
with some particular commodity named. And
if so, writers are bound so to express themselves as to convey to their readers, which of

* Dissertation on Value, c. ii. p. 58.
† Id. p. 39.

the two they intend to refer to. Whether these writers have chosen the very best terms to express these ideas is another question; but that the ideas themselves are quite different, and that it is essential to the language of political economy that they should be distinguished by different terms, cannot admit of a doubt. It appears to me, therefore, almost inconceivable that the author should say, " What information is conveyed, or what advance in argument is effected, by telling us, that value estimated in one way is real, but in another, is nominal?" It might as well be said, that, in speaking of our planetary system, no information is conveyed by using different adjuncts to the term distance, in order to distinguish between the distances of the planets from the sun, and the relations of their distances to each other. And supposing it had been the habit of most writers to call the first distances real and the second relative, would it not be most strange to say that the distinction in this way of distance into two kinds is incapable of being turned to any use, as all distance is relative?

The author is repeatedly dwelling upon the relative nature of value, as if he alone had considered it in this light ; but no other writer that I have met with has ever appeared to me to use the term value without an intelligible reference expressed or implied to something else ; and when the author says, in the passage above quoted, that value must always imply value in something which ought to be indicated, and that the terms nominal and real do not denote anything in this way, he appears to me, I own, to assert what is entirely without foundation. M. Say, for instance, in a passage quoted by the author in his notes,* observes, " There is this difference between a real and a relative variation of price ; that the former is a change of value arising from an alteration of the changes of production ; the latter a change arising from an alteration in the ratio of value of one particular commodity to other commodities. Now is it possible to say with truth, that the real and relative values here described do not both refer to other objects, and that these

* p. 240.

objects are not so different as to require to be distinguished?

The author may, perhaps, say, that if both expressions are meant to be relative, why use the terms real, positive, or absolute? The answer is, that the usage of our language allows it, and that nothing is more common than the use of the terms real, positive, and absolute, in contradistinction to relative, when the former terms have relation to some more general object, particularly to anything which is considered as a standard, whether accurate or inaccurate.

Thus, in the illustration before adverted to, although all distances are relative, it would be quite justifiable to say, that if the earth was moving towards the farthest part of her orbit, her positive, absolute, or real distance from the sun was increasing, although her distance relatively to that of some other planet or comet, moving from the sun with greater velocity, was diminishing. Tall and short, rich and poor, are relative terms: yet surely we should be warranted in saying, that Peter was not only taller than his three brothers, but, really or positively, a tall man. In the first case he is said to be tall in relation to three individuals ; but a stranger, knowing nothing of the height of these individuals, would obtain very little information from the statement. He would not know whether Peter was four feet, five feet, or six feet high : in the latter case, Peter is said to be tall in relation to the average or standard height of the race of men spoken of; and though the stranger might not have in his mind a perfectly accurate notion of this standard, yet he would immediately have before him the height of Peter within a few inches, instead of a few feet.

On the same principle, would it not be most ridiculous for any person gravely to propose that as rich and poor are relative terms, no one should ever call a man rich without mentioning at the same time the individual in relation to whom he was rich ? It is perfectly well known, that when, in any particular place or country, a man is said to be a rich man, the term refers to a sort of loose standard, expressing either a certain command over the goods of this life, or a certain superiority in this respect over the mass of the society, which superiority it had been the custom to mark by this expression. In either case, it would be allowable to call the man really or positively rich. But if the proposed change were adopted, and instead of saying that Mr. John Doe was a rich man, we could only say that he was rich in relation to Mr. Richard Roe, as poor Richard might be little better than a pauper, Mr. Doe might, after all, be in very narrow circumstances.

It is clear, therefore, not only that the terms real and positive may be legitimately applied in contradistinction to relative, when a relation to·some more general object or standard is intended ; but that the difference between the two sorts of relations is of the utmost importance, and ought to be carefully distinguished. It is not easy to conceive, therefore, how any writer could suppose that the language of political economy would be improved by a definition which would destroy this distinction, and make as many kinds of value as there are commodities, all equally real and equally nominal. In reference to

all other political economists, whenever they
have used the term value of a commodity,
without specifically mentioning the object in
which they intended to estimate it, I have
always felt myself authorised, consistently
with their general language, to consider them
as referring tacitly either to the mass of commodities, to the state of the supply compared
with the demand, or to the elementary costs
of production. But when the author of the
Critical Dissertation uses the term value,
which he does frequently without specific application, his general doctrine must leave the
reader quite at a loss to conjecture what he
means.

Proceeding on the same strange misapprehension or perversion of the language of
other writers, the author says of the writer of
the Templar's Dialogues, "Following Mr. Ricardo, he appears entirely to lose sight of the
relative nature of value, and, as I have remarked in the preceding chapter, to consider
it as something positive and absolute ; so that
if there were only two commodities in the
world, and they should both, by some circum-

stances or other, come to be produced by
double the usual quantity of labour, they
would both rise in real value, although their
relation to each other would be undisturbed.
According to this doctrine every thing might
at once become more valuable by requiring at
once more labour for its production ; a position utterly at variance with the truth, that
value denotes the relation in which commodities stand to each other as articles of exchange. Real value, in a word, is on this
theory considered as the independent result
of labour ; and, consequently, if under any
circumstances the quantity of labour is increased, the real value is increased. Hence
the paradox, that it is impossible for *a* continually to increase in value—in real value
observe, and yet command a continually decreasing quantity of *b*, and this although they
were the only two commodities in existence.
For it must not be supposed that the author
means that *a* might increase in value in
relation to a third commodity *c*, while it
commanded a decreasing quantity of *b ;* a

proposition which is too self-evident to be insisted on ; but he means that *a* might increase in a kind of value called real, which has no reference to any other commodity whatever. Apply to the position of this author the rule recommended in the last chapter ; inquire, when he speaks of value, value in what? and all the possible truth on the subject appears in its naked simplicity. He adds afterwards again, " value must be value in something, or in relation to something."*

Now let the reader recollect that this passage was written by a person who sets out with saying that value in its ultimate sense appears to mean the esteem in which any object is held, and it will appear most remarkable.

In the first place, what can the author possibly mean by speaking of the kind of value here called *real*, as if it had no relation to any thing else? The Templar, it must surely be allowed, has explained himself with sufficient

* Dissertation on Value, c. ii. p. 40.

clearness that by real value he means value in relation to the producing labour.

Secondly, I would ask the writer, who says that the value of a commodity means the esteem in which it is held, whether the labour required to produce a commodity does not, beyond all comparison, express more nearly the esteem in which the commodity is held, than a reference to some other commodity the producing labour of which is utterly unknown, and may therefore be one day or one thousand days?

I have already stated that I decidedly differ from Mr. Ricardo, and it follows of course that I differ equally from the Templar, in thinking that the value of a commodity may be correctly expressed by referring to the producing labour alone ; but compared with the expression of value proposed to be sub-stituted by the author of the Critical Disser-tation, it has a prodigious superiority. Let us try both, for instance, by the touch of the talisman recommended by the author himself. Let the question be the value of silver before the discovery of the American mines ; and let us ask, as directed, value in relation to what ? The Templar would answer, value in relation to the producing labour ; and though in this answer a material ingredient of elementary value is omitted, yet I should collect from it some tolerable notion of the esteem in which silver was held at that time ; and if I found, on comparison, that the producing labour was now three or four times less, I should be able, with tolerable certainty, to infer, that silver had grown more plentiful ; and that four centuries ago a given quantity of silver was held in much greater esteem, that is, people would make a much greater sacrifice in order to obtain it, than at present.

On the other hand, if the author of the Critical Dissertation should speak of the value of silver before the discovery of the American mines, and we should ask, value in relation to what ? the answer would be, " I have repeatedly stated that to know the value of an article at any period is merely to know its relation in exchange to some other commodity ;" consequently, we should know the

value of silver in the fifteenth century, or the
esteem in which it was held, by comparing
it with calicoes, although we might know
nothing at all about the difficulty or facility
of obtaining calicoes at that time. And if we
were to proceed, as in the former case, and,
with a view to ascertain the esteem in which
silver was held in the fifteenth century, as
compared with the esteem in which it is
held in the nineteenth, were to mark the relation of silver to calicoes in the two periods,
it would appear, that as, owing to the improvements in the cotton machinery, a given
quantity of silver would command more calicoes now than formerly, silver should be
considered as being held in higher estimation
now than four centuries ago.   Yet no person,
I believe, not even the author himself, would
agree to this conclusion. He would probably say that the comparison was merely
between silver and calicoes, and had nothing
to do with anything else. If this be all he
means, why does he confuse his readers by
stating that value means the esteem in which
a commodity is held ? and why does he say

that to know the value of an article at any
period is merely to know its relation in exchange to some other commodity ?   If all he
means by the value of a commodity is its relation to some other, why did he not at once
say, without ever talking about esteem, that
the value of one commodity in relation to
any other was expressed by the quantity of
that other for which the first would exchange ;
and that, when the first rose in relation to the
other, the other would always fall proportionably in relation to the first? If he had so
expressed himself, his proposition would have
obtained universal consent ; it would have
been a truism which had never been denied.
But as long as he continues to talk of the
esteem in which commodities are held, his
readers must consider him as peculiarly
inconsistent, if, on the supposition of there
being only two commodities in existence, he
prefers measuring the esteem in which one
of them is held by its relation to the other,
rather than by its relation to the producing
labour.   And they must further think, that
while he continues to state that " to know the

value of an article at any period is merely to know its relation in exchange to some other commodity," he is stating a proposition which, according to the usual sense in which the word value is understood when so placed, is totally unfounded. No man, I believe, but the author would venture to say that he should know the value of silver four hundred years ago by knowing the quantity of calicoes which an ounce of silver would then command.

The sixth chapter of the author is entitled " On Measures of Value ;" and the discussion of this subject leads him to such strange conclusions, that one cannot but feel the greatest surprise at his not seeing that he must have been proceeding in a wrong course. He ridicules the notion of its being necessary that a commodity should possess invariable value, in order to form a perfect measure of value. Such a notion, which he says in a note has been entertained by all the most distinguished writers in political economy, he civilly calls an utter absurdity. According to the doctrines and language of the author, no relation exists between the value of a commodity at one

time and the value of the same sort of commodity at another; and " the only use of a
measure of value, in the sense of a medium
of comparison, is between commodities existing at the same time."*

If this be so, it is, no doubt, quite absurd
in political economists to look for anything
approaching towards an invariable measure
of value, or even to talk of one commodity or
object being more steady or constant in its
value than another. At the same moment,
bags of hops are as good a measure of the
relative value of commodities as labour or
money. With regard to money, indeed, the
author particularly observes, that from the
relations between corn and money, at two
different periods, no other relation can be de-
duced; we do not advance a step beyond
the infirmation given. * * We cannot deduce
the relation of value between corn at the
first, and corn at the second period, because
no such relation exists, nor, consequently,
can we ascertain their comparative power
over other commodities. If we made the

* Dissertation on Value, c. vi. p. 117.

attempt, it would be, in fact, endeavouring to infer the quantities of corn which exchanged for each other at two different periods of time, a thing obviously absurd. And further, money would not be here discharging a particular function any more than the other commodity. We should have the value of corn in money and the value of money in corn, but one would be no more a measure or medium of comparison than the other."*

From all this it follows necessarily that we must on no account say, that butter has been rising during the last month ; if we do, we shall be convicted of the absurdity of proposing to exchange the butter which was consumed three weeks ago with the butter now on our table, in order to ascertain that a pound of the former will command less than a pound of the latter. For the same reason, we must not on any account say, that the value of wheat fell very greatly from 1818 to 1822, and rose considerably from 1822 to 1826. We must not venture to compare the value of the advances of a master manu

* Dissertation on Value, c. vi. p. 117.

facturer with the value of his returns ; or, in estimating the rate of his profits, presume to prefer money, which generally changes slowly and inconsiderably in its power of setting labour to work, to hops, which change so rapidly and greatly, &c. &c. In short, the whole of the language and inferences of the business of buying and selling, and making money, must be altered and adapted to the new definitions and doctrines.

It is quite astonishing that these consequences should not have startled the author, and made him turn back. If he had but adhered to his first description of value, namely, the esteem in which an object is held ; or even if he had interpreted his second definition of value, namely, " the power of purchasing other goods," according to the ordinary and natural meaning of the expression, he could never have been led into the strange mistake of supposing, that when people have talked of the value of a commodity at one period, compared with the value of the same kind of commodity at another, they could only refer to the rate at which they would actually exchange with each other, which, as no exchange could in such a case take place, would be absurd. What then did they mean? They obviously meant either to compare the esteem in which a commodity was held at one period with the esteem in which it was held at another, founded on the state of its supply compared with the demand, and ordinarily on its costs of production ; or to compare the general power of purchasing which a commodity possessed at one period with its general power of purchasing at another period. And will the author venture to assert, that there are not some objects better calculated than others to measure this esteem, or measure this general power of purchasing at different periods? Will the author maintain, that if, in reference to two periods in the same country, a commodity of a given kind will in the second period command double the quantity of labour that it did in the first, we could not with much more certainty infer that the esteem for it had greatly increased, than if we had taken calicoes or currants as the medium of comparison? Or would the author,

upon a little reflection, repeat again what he
says in the passage last quoted, that from the
relations between corn and money in two
successive seasons, we can deduce no other
relation, * * " money would not be here
discharging a particular function any more
than the other commodity. We should have
the value of corn in money and the value of
money in corn, but one would be no more a
measure or medium of comparison than the
other."*

To me, at least, these statements appear
utterly unfounded. If the money-price of
corn has risen this year to double what it was
in the last, I can infer, with almost absolute
certainty, that corn is held in much higher
estimation than it was. I can be quite sure
that the relation of corn to other articles, besides money, has most essentially changed,
and that a quarter of corn will now command
a much greater quantity of labour, a much
greater quantity of cloth, a much greater
quantity of hardware, a much greater quantity
of hats and shoes, than it did the year before :

* Dissertation on Value, c. vi. p. 117.

in short, that it will command nearly double
the quantity of all other commodities which
are in their natural and ordinary state, and
have not been essentially affected by the
causes which have operated upon the price
of corn.

Where then is the truth of saying, that from
the altered relation between corn and money
we deduce no other relation ? It is perfectly
obvious that we *can* deduce and *do* deduce a
great number of other most important relations ; and, in fact, *do* ascertain, though not
with perfect accuracy, yet with a most desirable and useful approach to it, the degree of
increase in the power of corn to command in
exchange the mass of other commodities.

On the other hand, from the diminished
power of money in relation to corn, we *cannot*
infer that money has fallen nearly in the same
proportion in relation to other commodities.
If an ounce of silver will now command only
half a bushel of wheat, instead of a whole
bushel, we can by no means infer that an
ounce of silver will therefore command only
about half the quantity of labour, half the

quantity of cloth, half the quantity of hardware, half the quantity of hats and shoes, and
of all those commodities which are in their
natural and ordinary state. To all these
objects money will probably bear nearly the
same relation as before.

Where, then, is the truth of saying, that
money would not be here discharging a particular function more than the other commodity? Broad, glaring, and incontrovertible
facts show, that for short periods money *does*
perform the function of measuring the variations in the general power of purchasing
possessed by the corn ; but that the corn does
not measure the variations in the general
power of purchasing possessed by the money.
This is one of the instances of that extraordinary inattention to facts which, most unfor-
tunately for the science of political economy,
the professors of it have lately indulged themselves in.

The author has said a great deal in good
set phrase about the false analogy involved
in the application of the term *measure* to the
value of commodities at different periods ; and

gravely states the difference between measuring length at different periods and measuring value.

I was not aware that people were ignorant
of this difference. As I said before, whenever mention is made of the value of a commodity at different periods, I have always
thought that a reference has been intended
either to its general power of purchasing, or
to something calculated to express the estimation in which it was held at these different
periods, founded on the state of its supply
compared with the demand, or the elementary
costs of its production.

But if the term has been generally understood in this way, people must have been
fully aware that value was essentially different
from length : they would know perfectly well
that a piece of cloth of a yard long would continue to be a yard long when it was sent to
China ; but that its value, that is, its general
power of purchasing in China, or the estimation in which it was held there, would probably be essentially altered. But allowing
this most marked distinction, and that the

value of a commodity cannot be so well defined, and its variations so accurately measured, as the length of a commodity—where
is the false analogy of endeavouring to measure these variations as well as we can ?   We
cannot certainly describe the wealth of a merchant, nor measure the increase of his wealth
during the last four years, with the same exactness as we can describe the height of a boy,
and measure the amount of his growth during
the same period.   We can perform the latter
operation with the most perfect precision by
means of a foot-rule.   The nature of wealth,
and the best instruments used to measure its
increase, are such, that the same precision is
unattainable ; but there is no false analogy
involved in the process of measuring the
wealth of a merchant at one time with his
wealth four years before, by the number of
pounds sterling which he possesses now, as
compared with the number of pounds sterling
he possessed at the former period.   What
false analogy is involved in applying money
to measure the value of the advances of a manufacturer, as compared with the value of his

returns, in order to estimate his profits? and
what can the author mean by saying, that no
relation of value can exist between commodities at different periods ;* and that it is a
case where money has no function to perform?

Notwithstanding such assertions, we see
every day the most perfect conviction prevailing among all agriculturists, merchants,
manufacturers, and shopkeepers, and among
all writers on political economy, except the
author, that to estimate the relation of commodities, at different periods, in regard to
their general power of purchasing, and particularly the power of purchasing labour,
the main instrument of production, is a most
important function, which it is peculiarly
desirable to have performed ; and that, for
moderately short periods, money *does* perform
this function with very tolerable accuracy.
And for this specific reason ; that, for moderately short periods, a given quantity of
money will represent, more nearly than any
other commodity, the general power of purchasing, and particularly the power of setting

* Dissertation on Value, c. vi. p. 113, et seq.

labour in motion, so vital to the capitalist. It will approach, in short, more nearly than any other commodity, to that invariability which the author thinks so utterly useless in a measure of value, and the very mention of which seems to excite his indignation.*

It is, in fact, by means of this same steadiness of value in the precious metals, which they derive from their great durability, and the consequent uniformity of their supply in the market, that they are enabled to perform their most important functions. Hops, or corn, as before stated, will measure the relative values of commodities at the same time and place; but let the author or reader attempt to estimate the profits of a capitalist in hops or corn, by the excess of the value of his advances above the value of his returns so estimated, and he will soon be bewildered. If a very plentiful year of corn were to succeed to a comparatively scarce one, the farmer, estimating both his outgoings and incomings in the corn of each year, might appear to gain above fifty per cent.,

* Dissertation on Value, c. vi. p. 110.

while, in reality, he might have lost, and might not be able, without trenching on his capital, to employ as many men on his farm as the year before. On the other hand, if a comparatively scarce year were to succeed to a plentiful one, his profits, estimated in corn, might appear to be less than nothing, and yet he might have been an unusual gainer, in reference to his general power of purchasing labour and other commodities, except corn. If the hop-planter were to estimate his advances and returns in hops, it is obvious that the results would be of the same kind, but aggravated in degree.

It must be allowed, then, that the commercial world have acted most wisely in selecting, for their practical measure of value, a commodity which is not only peculiarly convenient in its form, but is, in general, subject only to slow changes of value; and possesses, therefore, that steadiness in its power of purchasing labour and commodities, without which, all confidence in carrying on mercantile enterprises, of any duration, would be at an end.

But though the precious metals are a very useful and excellent measure of value for those periods, within which almost all mercantile transactions are begun and completed; yet, as Adam Smith very justly observes, they are not so for very long periods; not because there is no function for them to perform, but because, in the course of four hundred years, they are found to lose that uniformity of value, which, in general, they retain so well during four years.

I can by no means, therefore, agree with the author, when he says, speaking of the precious metals, that, " in regard to measuring or comparing value, there is no operation that can be intelligibly described, or consistently imagined, but may be performed by the media of which we are in possession."* Surely, to measure the relative power of a commodity over labour and the mass of other commodities, at different and distant times, is an operation which may be both consistently imagined, and intelligibly described; yet it is quite certain, that, in regard to dis-

* Dissertation on Value, c. vi. p. 102.

tant periods, the precious metals will not perform this well. Would the author himself venture to say, that the general power of purchasing possessed by an ounce of silver in the time of Edward the Third, was not very much greater than the general power of purchasing possessed by an ounce of silver in the time of George the Fourth; or, that the same quantity of agricultural labour, at these two periods, would not much more nearly have represented the same general power of purchasing? The author seems equally unfortunate when he launches out in praise of the precious metals as a measure of value, as when he says that they do not perform this function better than corn.

It will be observed that, in speaking of the values of commodities, at different periods, as meaning their different powers of purchasing at those periods, the kind of value referred to is, exclusively, value in exchange. And, in reference to value in exchange, exclusively, it appears to be of the utmost importance to the language of political economy, to distinguish between the power of purchasing generally, and the power of purchasing any one commodity.

But it must not be imagined that when the estimation in which a commodity is held at different periods is referred to, as determined at the time by the state of the supply compared with the demand, and ordinarily by the natural and necessary conditions of its supply, or by the elementary costs of its production, which are equivalent expressions, that value in exchange is lost sight of. Yet the author is continually falling into this kind of misapprehension, and into a total forgetfulness of his first account of the meaning of value, in his examination of Mr. Ricardo's views, as to the uses of a measure of value, in which, he says, a singular confusion of thought is to be discovered.*

Suppose, he observes, that we had such a commodity as Mr. Ricardo requires for a standard: suppose, for instance, all commodities to be produced by labour alone, and silver to be produced by an invariable quan-

* Dissertation on Value, c. vi. p. 120.

tity of labour. In this case, silver would be, according to Mr. Ricardo, a perfect measure of value. But in what sense? What is the function performed? Silver, even if invariable in its producing labour, will tell us nothing of the value of other commodities. Their relations in value to silver, or their prices, must be ascertained in the usual way; and, when ascertained, we shall certainly know the values of commodities in relation to each other; but in all this, there is no assistance derived from the producing labour of silver being a constant quantity."*

I have already described the function which silver would have to perform in this case, namely, either to measure the different powers of purchasing possessed by commodities at different periods, or to measure the different degrees of estimation in which they were held at these different periods.

Now, in the first place, with regard to the general power of purchasing, can it be denied for a moment, that, granting all the premises, as the author does hypothetically, silver, so

* Dissertation on Value, c. vi. p. 122.

produced, would be, beyond comparison, a
better measure of the power of purchasing
generally, than silver as it has been actually
produced? It would be secured from that
greatest source of variation in the general
power of purchasing occasioned by the variation in its own producing labour; and an
ounce of such silver would command much
more nearly the same quantity of labour and
commodities, for four or five hundred years
together, than an ounce of silver derived
from mines of greatly varying fertility.

Secondly, with regard to the estimation in
which a commodity is held, it is not easy to
conceive a more complete measure. If all
commodities were produced by labour alone,
and exchanged with each other according to
the producing labour; and if silver were
produced by an invariable quantity of labour,
the quantity of silver given for a commodity
in the market at different periods, would
express almost accurately the relative estimation in which it was held at these periods;
because it would express at once the relative
sacrifice which people were willing to make,

in order to obtain such a commodity at these
different periods; the relative conditions of
the supply, or elementary costs of production, of such commodity at these periods;
and the proportion of the produce to the
producer, or the relative state of the demand,
as compared with the supply of such commodity at these different periods. And if the
value of a commodity means, as the author
has told us in the first sentence of his book,
the esteem in which it is held, Mr. Ricardo's
measure would certainly do all which he proposed it should do; and this specifically on
account of its invariability in relation to the
estimation in which it was held.

It would not merely indicate, as the author
states, in which of two commodities varying
in relation to each other, at different periods,
the variation had taken place;* but it would
express the precise amount of the variation;
that is, if it appeared by documents that the
price of a yard of cloth of a certain quality
four hundred years ago was twenty shillings,
and its price at present was only ten shillings,

* Dissertation on Value, c. vi. p. 121.

it would follow, that the estimation in which it was held, or its value, had fallen one-half; because, as all commodities are, by the supposition, produced by labour alone, the sacrifice with which it could be obtained, the necessary conditions of its supply, or the elementary costs of its production, had diminished one-half.

The variations of a commodity, in relation to this kind of standard, would further show, with great exactness, the variations in its power of commanding all those commodities which had not altered in the conditions of their supply, or the elementary costs of production. If a commodity rose or fell in this standard price, at different periods, it would necessarily rise or fall exactly in the same proportion in its power of commanding, in exchange, all those commodities which had not altered in the conditions of their supply, or their elementary costs of production.

But still, it will be readily acknowledged, that, even granting all that the author has granted hypothetically to Mr. Ricardo, it is not true that such silver would be an *accurate* measure of the general power of purchasing. Although the circumstance of its invariability, in regard to its producing labour, would give it a prodigious superiority over all other commodities even in this respect, yet, as the producing labour of many commodities may vary in the progress of society, it is quite impossible that the same quantity of any one object can, through successive periods, represent the same general power of purchasing. This is universally allowed; and as it would be clearly desirable to have *one* rather than *two* definitions of value, the question is, whether, both on this account, and on account of the universal language and practice of society, for short periods, it would not be decidedly better to confine the term value of a commodity, when used generally, to the estimation in which it is held, determined by the state of the supply compared with the demand, and ordinarily by the elementary costs of production, rather than to its general power of purchasing. There is very nearly an accurate measure of

the former; it is universally acknowledged
that there cannot be an accurate measure of
the latter; and further, it is most important
to remark that, in adopting the former, our
language would much more nearly coincide
with the ordinary language of society in referring to variations of value, than if we
adopted the latter.

As a matter of fact, when a rise in the
value of hops or of corn is spoken of, who
ever thinks about the changes which may
have taken place in the values of iron, flax,
or cabbages? For short periods, we consider
money as nearly a correct measure of the
values of commodities, as well as of their
prices; and if hops and corn have risen in
this measure, we do not hesitate to say that
their values have risen, without the least
reference to cloths, calicoes, or cambrics.
This is a clear proof that, in general, when
we speak of the variations in the values of
commodities, we do not measure them by
the variations in their general power of purchasing, but by some sort of standard which
we think better represents the varying esti-

mation in which they are held, determined at all times by the state of the supply compared with the demand, and, on an average, by the elementary costs of production.

The only variations in the general power of a commodity to purchase, which are susceptible of a distinct and definite measure, are those which arise from causes which affect the commodity itself, and not from the causes which affect the innumerable articles against which it is capable of being exchanged. In speaking, therefore, of the variations in the value of particular commodities, it is not only more accordant with the accustomed meaning attached to the expression, but absolutely necessary with a view to precision, to consider them as exclusively proportioned to, and measured by, the amount of the causes of value operating upon themselves.

Mr. Ricardo, therefore, quite consistently with his own hypothesis, considers a commodity, the producing labour of which has doubled, as having increased to double its former value. It has increased in relation to a standard which, according to him, is the sole cause of value ; it will command just double the quantity of all those commodities which have not altered in their producing value ; and if it will not command just double the quantity of other commodities, it is not because it will not command just double the *value* which it did before, but because, on account of the changes in the producing labour of the other commodities, double the quantity of them has become more or less than double the value.

On the same principle, Adam Smith considers the value of cattle as rising in the progress of cultivation and improvement, although the value of land, the value of wood, the value of poultry, &c., might rise still higher, and, consequently, a given quantity of cattle might, with regard to some commodities or sets of commodities, have its power of purchasing diminished. But in saying that the value of cattle rises in the progress of cultivation, he means to say, that it rises in relation to a standard, namely, the labour a commodity will command, which represents

at different periods the state of the supply of
cattle compared with the demand, and, on an
average, the elementary costs of their production ; and, consequently, much better
represents the estimation in which they are
held than any commodity or set of commodities. " Labour," he observes, " it must
always be remembered, and not any particular commodity, or set of commodities, is
the real measure of the value both of silver
and of all other commodities."*

Even the author himself has a chapter on
the causes of value ; and here he finds it
absolutely necessary to estimate the causes
affecting one commodity as distinct from the
causes affecting another ; although, according to his previous doctrine, the value of
one commodity might be just as powerfully
affected by causes operating upon another
commodity as by causes operating upon itself.
If a and b be compared, the value of a will
be equally doubled, whether the elementary
cost of a be doubled or the elementary cost
of b be diminished one half ; and so no doubt

* Wealth of Nations, b. i. c. xi. p. 291, 6th edit.

it would, if the relation of a to b were alone
considered. But what does this prove? not
that the value of a is not very differently
affected in the two cases, according to the
most ordinary, the most useful, and the most
correct acceptation of the term value ; but
that to confine the term value, as the author
does, to the mere relation of any one commodity to any other, is to render it pre-eminently futile and useless.

In first separating value in exchange from
value in use, it may be allowable to distinguish it by the title of the power of purchasing other goods, as Adam Smith has
done, though never to interpret this power
as the power of purchasing any one sort of
goods, as the author has done. But the moment we come to inquire into the variations
of the values of commodities at different
periods, we must, with any view to precision
and utility, draw a marked line of distinction
between a variation in the power of purchasing derived from causes affecting the
particular purchasing commodities, and the
variations in the power of purchasing which

may arise from causes operating upon the purchased commodities. We must confine our attention exclusively to the former ; and for this purpose refer to some standard which will best enable us to estimate the variations in the elementary costs of production, and in the state of the demand and supply of these commodities, as the best criterion of their varying value, or the varying estimation in which they are held at different periods.

On these grounds, Mr. Ricardo, consistently with his peculiar theory, measures the varying values of commodities at different periods by their producing labour.

And Adam Smith, consistently with his more just and applicable theory, measures the values of commodities at different periods by the labour which they will command.

Among the author's chapters is one (the seventh) entitled " On the Measure of Value proposed by Mr. Malthus."

In order to prepare himself for the refutations intended, he sums up his principal doctrines respecting value ; and as they are here brought into a small compass, I cannot resist the temptation of quoting them in his own words.

He says, " It has been shown that the value of labour, like that of any other exchangeable article, is denoted by the quantity of some other commodity for which a definite portion of it will exchange, and must rise or fall as that quantity becomes greater or smaller, these phrases being only different expressions of the same event. Hence, unless labour always exchanges for the same quantity of other things, its value cannot be invariable, and, consequently, the very supposition of its being, at one and the same time, invariable, and capable of measuring the variations of other commodities, involves a contradiction."

" It has also been shown, that to term anything immutable in value, amidst the fluctuations of other things, implies that its value at one time may be compared with its value at another time, without reference to any other commodity, which is absurd, value denoting a relation between two things at the same time ; and it has likewise been shown, that in no sense could an object of invariable value be of any peculiar service in the capacity of a measure.

"These considerations," he says, " are quite sufficient to overturn the claims of the proposed measure, as maintained by its advocate."*

I am most ready to acknowledge that they are amply sufficient for the purpose, if they are true. But is it possible that doctrines can be true, which, having no other foundation than a most arbitrary and unwarranted interpretation of a definition of Adam Smith, lead directly to the subjoined conclusions?

First; That the value of labour rises or falls as a given portion of it will exchange for a greater or less quantity of silk or any other commodity, however unconnected with the labourer's wants; so that if silks were to fall to one-half their price, the value of labour would be doubled.

Secondly; That the value of corn in one year cannot be compared with the value of corn in another, because value denotes

* Dissertation on Value, c. vii. p. 140.

only a relation between two things at the same time.

And thirdly, That the comparative steadiness in the value of the precious metals, for short periods, is of no service to them in the capacity of a measure of value.

The decision of the question, as to the truth of doctrines necessarily leading to such conclusions, may be safely left to the reader. But to return to the main subject of the chapter, namely, the measure of value proposed by me.

In a publication entitled " *The Measure of Value stated and illustrated*," I had given reasons, which appeared to me convincing, for adopting labour, in the sense in which it is generally understood and applied by Adam Smith, as the measure of value ; and further to illustrate the subject, and bring into one view the results of different suppositions respecting the varying fertility of the soil and the varying quantity of corn paid to the labourer, I added a table in which different suppositions of this kind are made.

In reference to this table the author ob-

serves, that " In the same way any article
might be proved to be of invariable value,
for instance, ten yards of cloth. For whether
we gave 5*l*. or 10*l*, for the ten yards, the sum
given would always be equal in value to the
cloth for which it was paid, or, in other words,
of invariable value in relation to cloth. But
that which is given for a thing of invariable
value must itself be invariable, whence the
ten yards of cloth must be of invariable
value."*

This comparison shows either a most singular want of discrimination, or a purposed
disregard of the premises on which the table
is founded. These premises are, that the
natural and necessary conditions of the supply
of the great mass of commodities, or, in other
words, their elementary costs of production,
are, the accumulated and immediate labour
necessary to produce them, with the addition
of the ordinary profits upon the whole
advances for the time they have been
advanced; and that the ordinary values
of commodities at different periods, accord-

* Dissertation on Value, c. vi. p. 145.

ing to the most customary application of the
term, are determined by the elementary costs
of production at those periods, that is,
by the labour and profits worked up in
them.

If these premises be just, the table correctly
illustrates all that it was intended to illustrate. If the premises be false, the whole
falls to the ground.

Now, I would ask the author, what sort of
resemblance there is between ten yards of
cloth and ten days' labour? Is cloth the
universal and the main instrument of production? Is the advance of an adequate
quantity of cloth the natural and necessary
condition of the supply of all commodities?
Has any one ever thought of calling cloth and
profits the elementary costs of production?
or has it ever been proposed to estimate the
values of commodities at different periods by
the different quantities of cloth and profits
worked up in them?

If these questions cannot be answered in
the affirmative, it is obvious that what may be
true and important with regard to labour, may

be perfectly false or futile in regard to any *product* of labour.* The whole depends upon the mode of estimating the values of commodities.

It would, no doubt, be an absurd tautological truism merely to state, that the varying wages of a given quantity of labour will always command the same quantity of labour ; but if it were previously shown that the quantity of labour which a commodity commands represents exactly the quantity of labour

---

* It has always been a matter of great surprise to me that I should have been accused of *arbitrarily* adopting labour as the measure of value. If there be not a most marked and characteristic distinction between labour and any *product* of labour, I do not know where a characteristic distinction between two objects is to be found ; and surely I have stated this distinction often enough, and brought forward the peculiar qualities of labour as my reasons for thinking that it may be taken as a measure of value. Opinions may differ as to the sufficiency of these reasons, or as to the degree of accuracy with which it will serve the purpose of a measure. But how it can be said that I have adopted it arbitrarily, is quite unintelligible to me. If I had merely stated, that I had adopted it because it was the main element in the natural costs of production, there could have been no ground for such a charge.

worked up in it, with the profits upon the advances, and does therefore really represent and measure those natural and necessary conditions of the supply, those elementary costs of production which determine value ; then the truism that the varying wages of a given quantity of labour always command the same quantity of labour, must necessarily involve the important truth, that the elementary costs of producing the varying wages of a given quantity of labour must always be the same.

It is obvious to any person inspecting the table, that the uniform numbers in the seventh column, illustrating the invariable value of the wages of a given number of men, might, with perfect certainty, have been stated without the intermediate steps ; but if they had been so stated, no conclusion respecting the constancy of the value of such wages could have been drawn. The intermediate steps, which show that the value of the wages of ten men is there estimated by the causes which had been previously shown to determine the values of all commodities, can alone warrant the conclusion that the uniform numbers in the seventh column imply uniformity of value in the wages.

Mr. Ricardo had stated repeatedly, that the value of the wages of labour must necessarily rise in the progress of society. He builds, indeed, the whole foundation of his theory of profits on the rise and fall of the value of labour. The table shows that, if we estimate the value of wages by the labour worked up in them, that is, by one element of value, Mr. Ricardo is right, and the value of wages will really rise as poorer land is taken into cultivation; but that, if we estimate the value of wages by the labour and *profits* worked up in them, that is, by the two elementary ingredients of value, the value of wages will remain the same.

The author says that, from the remarks he has made, the reader will perceive that Mr. Malthus's " Table illustrating the invariable value of labour," absolutely proves nothing ;* and he concludes his chapter with observing, that his " cursory review evinces that the

* Dissertation on Value, c. vii. p. 148.

formidable array of figures in the table yields not a single new or important truth.*

I was not aware that it was ever expected from a tabular arrangement, that it should afford logical proofs of new propositions; but, if the author means that, taking the whole publication together, it contains nothing new or important, though I may be bound to believe it in relation to his own reading and his own views, I cannot help doubting it a little in regard to the reading and views of many others; and I am quite certain that, with regard to myself, the view I there took of the subject of value, and of the reasons for adopting labour as its measure, was, in many of its parts, quite new to me a year before the publication.

In the first place; I had nowhere seen it stated, that the ordinary quantity of labour which a commodity will command must represent and measure the quantity of labour worked up in it, with the addition of profits. But, as soon as my attention was strongly drawn to his truth, the labour which a com-

* Dissertation on Value, c. vii. p. 150.

modity would ordinarily command appeared
to me in a new light. I had before considered labour as the most general and the
most important of all the objects given in
exchange, and, therefore, by far the best
measure of the general power of purchasing
of any one object ; but after I became aware
that, by representing the labour worked up in
a commodity, with the profits, it represented
the natural and necessary conditions of its
supply, or the elementary costs of its production, its importance, as a measure, appeared to me very greatly increased.

Secondly ; I had nowhere seen it stated
that, however the fertility of the soil might
vary, the elementary costs of producing the
wages of a given quantity of labour must
always necessarily be the same. Colonel
Torrens, in adverting to a measure of value,
says, " In the first place, exchangeable value
is determined by the cost of production ; and
there is no commodity, the cost of producing
which is not liable to perpetual fluctuation.
In the second place, even if a commodity
could be found which always required the

same expenditure for its production, it would not, therefore, be of invariable exchangeable value, so as to serve as a standard for measuring the value of other things. Exchangeable value is determined, not by the absolute, but by the relative, cost of production."*

I had been convinced, however, that, with a view to superior accuracy and utility, and a more complete conformity to the language and practice of society, in estimating the varying values of commodities for short periods, it was necessary to separate the variations in the power of a commodity to purchase, into two parts; the first, derived from causes operating upon the commodity itself; the second, from causes operating upon other commodities; and, in speaking of the variations in the exchangeable value of a commodity, to refer only to the former. In this case it is obvious that, according to Colonel Torrens, we should possess a measure of value if we could find an object the cost of producing which was always the same.

* On the Production of Wealth, c. i. p. 56.

Now it is shown, in the " *Measure of value stated and illustrated*," that the conditions of the supply of labour, or the elementary costs of producing the corn wages of a given number of men, estimated just in the same way as we should estimate the elementary costs of producing cloth, linens, hardware, or any other commodity, must of necessity always remain the same.

I own that these two necessary qualities of the labour, which commodities will *ordinarily* command, were practically new to me ; and, when forced on my attention, and accompanied by the conviction above described, as to the most correct and useful definition of value, made me view labour as a measure of value, so far approaching towards accuracy, considering the nature of the subject, that it might fairly be called a standard.

The publication was also marked by another peculiarity, which I cannot but consider as of some importance : namely, the constant use of the term *labour and profits*, instead of the customary one, *labour and capital*.

It must be allowed that the expression

labour and capital is essentially tautological. In every definition of capital I have met with, the means of commanding labour are included; and there can be no doubt that machinery and raw materials require labour for their production of the same general description, and usually in as large a proportion, as the labour advanced by the last capitalist. Speaking loosely, we may indeed use the expression *labour and capital*, meaning by capital, when so used, all that part of the general description of capital which does not consist of the means of commanding the immediate labour required. But when we are engaged in an inquiry into the elements of value, nothing can be more unphilosophical than to talk of labour and capital. Excluding rent and taxes, the only elements concerned in regulating the value of commodities are labour and profits, including, of course, in such labour, the labour worked up in the raw materials, and that portion of the machinery worn out in the production; and including in the profits, the profits of the producers of the raw materials and machinery.

To say that the values of commodities are regulated or determined by the *quantity* of *capital and labour* necessary to produce them is essentially false. To say that the values of commodities are regulated by the quantities of labour *and profits* necessary to produce them is, I believe, essentially true. And if so, it was a point of some importance to substitute the expression *labour and profits* for the customary one of *labour and capital.*

I have been detained longer than I intended by the Critical Dissertation on the Nature, Measures, and Causes of Value. There is still matter of animadversion remaining; but were I to go on I should tire my readers, if I have not done it already.

The author, when not under the influence of his peculiar definitions, makes some very just observations; and the work is exceedingly well written; which makes it a matter of greater surprise that its main proposition should be so strikingly adverse to the principle of utility, and so peculiarly calculated to retard the progress of that science which it must have been intended to promote.

I do not think it necessary to the object I have in view, to proceed further with these remarks on the definition and use of terms among political economists. What I have already said, if just, will be sufficient to show that much uncertainty has arisen from our* negligence on this important point, and much improvement might be expected from greater attention to it. I shall now, therefore, proceed to define some of the principal terms in political economy, as nearly as I can, according to the rules laid down. But before I begin, I think it may be useful to give a summary of the reasons for adopting the subjoined definition of the measure of value.

* I am very ready to include myself among those political economists who have not been sufficiently attentive to this subject.

CHAPTER IX.

SUMMARY OF THE REASONS FOR ADOPTING THE SUB-JOINED DEFINITION OF THE MEASURE OF VALUE.

As a preliminary, it may be proper to state, that it seems absolutely essential to the language of political economy, that the expression *value of a commodity*, like the expression *price of a commodity*, should have some fixed and determined sense attached to it. Every person who has either written or talked on the subject of political economy, has been constantly in the habit of using the term without specifically expressing the object of comparison intended: and if it were true, that we might with equal propriety suppose any one of a thousand different objects referred to, it might easily be shown, that all past writers who had used the term value had talked the greatest nonsense; and all future writers must abound in the most tedious circumlocutions and the most futile propositions.

But the author of the Critical Dissertation on Value has certainly done injustice to the writers who have gone before him, in supposing that when they have used the term value of a commodity, no reference was implied, if it was not expressed. As I stated before, they must be considered as referring, in some form or other, either to its general power of purchasing, or, to the estimation in which it was held, determined by the state of its supply compared with the demand, and, on an average, by the elementary costs of production; and as it would be perfectly ridiculous to suppose, that when the values of commodities, at different periods, are spoken of generally, by respectable writers, they could mean to refer to individual commodities not intended to represent, more or less accurately, the above objects of reference; it is obvious, that the ultimate reference implied must be confined to one of these, or their equivalents.

I have already given my reasons for thinking it more correct and useful to refer to the estimation in which a commodity is held,

determined as above described, rather than
to its general power of purchasing; but, as
others may be of a different opinion, it may
be useful to include among the reasons for
adopting labour as a measure of value, its
qualities as a measure of the general power
of purchasing.

Supposing, then, that the exchangeable
value of a commodity were defined to be its
general power of purchasing, this must refer
to the power of purchasing the mass of
commodities; but this mass is quite unma-
nageable, and the power of purchasing it
can never be ascertained. With a view,
therefore, to its practical application, it would
unquestionably be our endeavour to fix upon
some object, or set of objects, which would
best represent an average of the general mass.
Now, of any one object, it cannot for a moment
be denied that labour best represents an
average of the general mass of productions.
There is no commodity considered by society
as wealth, for which labour is not, in the first
instance, exchanged; there are very few for
which it is not exchanged in great quantities:

and this can be said of no other object,
except labour, and the circulating medium
which represents it. It is, at once, the first,
the universal, and the most important object
given in exchange for all commodities; and
if to this we add, that while there is one large
class of commodities, such as raw products,
which in the progress of society tends to rise
as compared with labour, there is another
large class of commodities, such as manufactured articles, which at the same time tends
to fall; it may not be far from the truth
to say, that the portion of the average mass
of commodities which a given quantity of
labour will command in the same country,
during the course of some centuries, may not
very essentially vary.

Allowing, however, that it would vary, and
that labour is an imperfect measure of the
general power of purchasing; yet, if some
sort of standard more applicable than the
mass of commodities be required, and labour
appears to be beyond comparison the best
representative of this mass, there will be
a very powerful reason for adopting labour

as the practical measure of value, even among those who may persevere in thinking that the best definition of value in exchange is the general power of purchasing.

To those, however, who hold the opinion that the variations in the exchangeable value of a commodity and the variations in its power of purchasing are not identical, and that a commodity increases in exchangeable value only when it will command a *greater value in exchange*, while its power of purchasing may increase merely because it will command a *greater quantity* of commodities which have confessedly fallen in value, the reasons for adopting labour as the measure of value will be found to increase tenfold in force.

There are various ways of describing value in the sense here understood ; and the slightest examination of them will show that the labour which a commodity will command can alone be the measure of such value.

First; The author of the Critical Dissertation on Value has commenced his work by a description of it, in which I entirely agree with him. He says, as I have before stated, that " value, in its ultimate sense, appears to mean the esteem in which any object is held. But it is obvious that the degree of this esteem cannot be measured by comparing it with another commodity about which we know as little as of the first. The comparison with money would leave us as much in the dark as ever, if we did not previously know the estimation in which money was held.* Even the mere *relative* values of two commodities cannot be inferred by putting them side by side, and looking at them for any length of time. Before we can attain even this partial conclusion, we must refer each of them to the desires of man, and the means of production ; that is, we must make a previous comparison, in order to ascertain the value of each before we can venture to say what relation one bears to the other. It is this primary comparison which, indepen-

---

* If in a foreign country, in which the relation of money to men and labour was unknown to us, we were told that a quarter of corn was selling for four ounces of silver, we should not know whether there was a famine, and corn was held in the highest estimation, or whether there was a glut of corn, and it was held in the lowest estimation. The very term estimation, as applied to commodities, must of necessity refer to man and labour.

dently of any secondary comparison, determines the estimation in which the commodity
is held. And as this primary comparison can
only be represented by the exchange with labour, it is certain that, if we define the value
of a commodity to be the estimation in which
it is held, the quantity of labour which it will
command can alone measure this estimation.

Secondly : Locke, most justly looking to the
foundation of all value, considers the value
of commodities as determined by the proportion of their quantity to their vent, or of
the supply to the demand ; but the varying
vent or demand for one commodity cannot
possibly be represented by the varying quantity of another commodity for which it is exchanged, unless the second commodity remain
steady in regard to labour. If at one time I
give two pounds of hops for a yard of cloth,
and at another time only one, it does not
at all follow that the demand for cloth has
diminished ; on the contrary, it may be increased, and in giving the value of one pound
of hops, I may have enabled the cloth manufacturer to set more men to work, and to

obtain higher profits than when I gave the value of two pounds. But the demand for a commodity, though not proportioned to the *quantity* of any other commodity which the purchaser is willing and able to give for it, is really proportioned to *the quantity of labour* which he will give for it ; and for this reason : the quantity of labour which a commodity will *ordinarily* command, represents exactly the effectual demand for it ; because it represents exactly that quantity of labour and profits united necessary to effect its supply ;* while the *actual* quantity of labour which a commodity will command when it differs from the *ordinary* quantity, represents the excess or defect of demand arising from temporary causes. If then looking to the foundation of all value, namely, the limitation

It is a truth fruitful in important consequences, that the labour which commodities will command when in their natural state, by representing accurately the quantity of labour and profits necessary to produce them, must represent accurately the effectual demand for them. And this holds good at different places and times, referring of course to the labour of the same description at each place and time.

of the supply as compared with the wants of mankind, we consider the value of commodities at any time or place as proportioned to the state of their supply compared with the demand at that time and place, it is evident that the quantity of labour of the same time and place which any commodity, or parcels of commodities, will command, can alone represent and measure the state of the supply of them as compared with the demand,* and their values as founded on this relation.

Thirdly: It has often been stated that the value of a commodity is determined by the sacrifice which people are willing to make in order to obtain it ; and this seems to be perfectly true. But the question recurs, how are we to measure this sacrifice ? It is obvious that we cannot measure it by the *quantity* of another commodity which we are willing to give in exchange for it. When I give more calicoes, or more potatoes, than I did before, for a certain quantity of hardware, it does not

---

* What could give us any information respecting the scarcity of a commodity in China, or the state of its supply as compared with the demand, but a reference to Chinese labour ?

at all follow that I make a greater sacrifice in order to obtain what I want. On the contrary, if calicoes and potatoes had both fallen in price, the one from improved machinery and the other from the abundance of the season, my sacrifice might even have been less rather than greater. Even the quantity of money which is given for a commodity is no measure of the sacrifice made to obtain it. Though it is an excellent measure of the variations in the sacrifice made, at the same time and place; yet without further information, it will tell us nothing either about the amount, or the variations at different places and times. The giving of an ounce of silver was a very different sacrifice in the time of Edward I. from what it is at present. It is obvious, therefore, that the sacrifice which we are willing to make, in order to obtain a particular commodity, is not proportioned to the *quantity* of any other commodity for which it will exchange, but to the difficulty with which such quantity, whether more or less, is attained. Now labour can measure this difficulty, but nothing else can. If, then, the value of a commodity be determined by the sacrifice which people are willing to make in order to obtain it, it is the labour given for a commodity, and labour alone, which can measure this sacrifice.

Fourthly : In the *Measure of Value Stated and Illustrated,* I considered the value of commodities as, on an average, determined by the natural and necessary conditions of their supply. These conditions I stated to be the accumulated and immediate labour worked up in commodities with the ordinary profits upon the whole advances for the time that they were advanced. And it appeared, both in the early part of the discussion, and in the Table, that the quantity of labour which a commodity would ordinarily command must represent and measure the quantity of labour worked up in it with the addition of profits. It was certainly a very remarkable fact, that when Mr. Ricardo chose the labour worked up in commodities " as, under many circumstances, an invariable standard," and rejected the labour which they would ordinarily purchase as subject to as many fluctuations as the commodities compared with it,* he should not have seen that the labour which a commodity will ordinarily command, necessarily involves his own proposition, with that addition to it merely which can alone make it correct; and that it is precisely because the labour which a commodity will ordinarily command measures the labour actually worked up in it with the addition of profits, that it is justifiable to consider it as a measure of value. If then the ordinary value of a commodity be considered as determined by the natural and necessary conditions of its supply, it is certain that the labour which it will ordinarily command is alone the measure of these conditions.

Fifthly: The values of commodities are often said to be determined by the costs of production. When the costs of production do not refer to money, but to those simple elements of production, without an adequate quantity of which, whatever may be their price in money, the commodity cannot be produced, they are precisely the same as the

* Principles of Polit. Econ., c. i. s. i. p. 5. 3d edit.

natural and necessary conditions of the supply.
The elementary costs of production, excluding
rents and taxes, are the labour and profits
required to produce a commodity. Of these
it has been already shown, that the labour
which the commodity will ordinarily command is alone the measure ; and allowing
that we could obtain with tolerable exactness
the average price of common agricultural
labour at different times and in different
countries, and that when the prices of all
other sorts of labour were once established,
they would (as assumed by Adam Smith
and Mr. Ricardo) continue to bear nearly
the same relation to each other in the
further progress of cultivation and improvement, it is certain that the quantity of common agricultural labour which a commodity
would ordinarily command at any place and
time would measure, with a near approach to
accuracy, the elementary costs of production
at that place and time ; so that commodities,
which at two different periods in the same
country wuld ordinarily command the same
quantity of agricultural labour, might fairly

be said to be equal to each other in their elementary costs of production, and, of course, in their values, if their values be determined by their elementary costs of production.

Sixthly : It may be said that the value of a commodity must be proportioned to its supply compared with the number of its producers. This appears, indeed, to be strikingly the case in the early periods of society when many commodities are obtained, almost exclusively, by labour. If fruits are to be procured, or game killed or caught, by labour alone, or assisted only by capital of very little value, the quantity obtained, on an average, by a day's labour must represent, with a great approach to accuracy, the degree of scarcity in which commodities exist compared with the producers of them working for a certain time. But the degree in which the supply of a commodity is limited, as compared with the numbers, powers, and wants of those who wish to obtain it, is the foundation of all value. Here the producers are both the effectual demanders and the consumers ; and the produce obtained on an average by a single

producer must represent the supply compared
with the numbers, powers, and wants of the
demanders. If a large quantity of produce
be obtained by a producer, the commodity
will be in abundance, and will be considered
as of comparatively little value ; if a small
quantity be obtained by a producer, the commodity will be scarce, and will be considered
as of comparatively great value. If it be the
custom of the country for the producers to
work only four hours a-day instead of ten or
twelve, the commodities produced will bear a
comparatively small proportion to the numbers of the producers and effectual demanders,
and will consequently be of much higher
value, than in those countries where it is the
custom to work for the greater number of
hours ; and, on the other hand, if the producers, besides working ten or twelve hours
a-day, are aided by ingenious instruments and
great skill in the use of them, the commodities produced will be in unusual plenty compared with the producers, and will be considered as proportionally of low value. In all
these cases the value of the commodity is

evidently determined by the relation between its quantity and the number of its producers.

Now though, in the more advanced stages of society, the producer is not always at the same time the demander and consumer; yet the effectual demand for commodities must, on an average, be proportioned to the productive services set in motion to obtain them;* and when the different kinds of producers are reduced to a common denominator, such as common agricultural day-labour, and profits. are deducted as the remuneration of the capitalist, and rent as the remuneration of the landowner, the proportion which the remaining produce bears to the number of such producers must represent, exactly in the same manner as in the early periods of society, the degree of scarcity in which the commodity exists compared with the producers; and therefore the value of the commodity is measured by the quantity of it which will command a day's common labour. In fact, if it

* M. Say's comprehensive expression, " *Services productifs,*" includes profits and rents as well as labour; but it is certain that labour will measure accurately the value of the whole amount of these services.

be once allowed that when labour is exclusively concerned, the number of days' labour
necessary to produce a commodity at any
place and time represents the natural value of
the commodity at that place and time*, then,
as it is quite certain that the value in exchange
of any other commodity compared with the
first, will be accurately in proportion to the
respective quantities of the same kind of
labour which they will command, it follows
necessarily, that the value of the second commodity must always be in proportion to the
quantity of labour it will command, however
its value may have been affected by profits,
rents, taxes, monopolies, or the accidental
state of its supply compared with the demand.

Seventhly: It has been stated that the
values of commodities must be proportioned
to the causes of value operating upon them.
The author of the Critical Dissertation has a
chapter on the causes of value, and, at the
conclusion of it, adverting to the variety of
considerations operating upon the human

* If this concession be once made, the whole question respecting labour as a measure of value is at once
decided.

mind, which he thinks have been overlooked by political economists, he observes, " these considerations are the causes of value ; and the attempt to proportion the quantities in which commodities are exchanged for each other to the degree in which one of these considerations exists, must be vain and ineffectual. All, in reality, that can be accomplished on this subject, is to ascertain the various causes of value ; and, when this is done, we may always infer, from an increase or diminution of any of them, an increase or diminution of the effect."*

These remarks, it must be allowed, are justly applicable to those who propose to measure the values of commodities by the quantity of labour actually bestowed upon them ; but in no degree to those who propose to measure them by the quantity of labour which they will command. We have already shown that the labour which commodities will command measures that paramount cause of value which includes every other ; namely, the state of the supply as compared

* c. xi. p. 232.

with the demand. Whatever may be the
number and variety of considerations operating on the mind in the interchange of
commodities, whether merely the common
elementary costs of production, or whether
these costs have been variously modified by
taxes, by portions of rent, by monopolies
strict or partial, and by temporary scarcity
or abundance, the result of the whole must
appear in the state of the supply compared
with the demand ; and in the case of an
individual article, the supply of which may
be considered as given, the demand must be
proportioned to the sacrifice which the purchasers are able and, under all the circumstances, willing to make in order to attain it.

But it has already been shown that it is
the command of labour which the purchasers
are able and willing to transfer to the sellers,
and not any particular commodity, except in
proportion as it will command labour, that
can alone represent the sacrifice of the purchasers. The labour, therefore, which a
commodity will command, or which the purchasers are willing to give for it, measures

the result of all the causes of value acting
upon it,—of all the various considerations
operating upon the mind in the interchange
of commodities.

Whether then we consider the value of a
commodity at any place and time as expressed
by the estimation in which it is held; whether
we consider it as founded entirely on the
state of the supply as compared with the
demand; whether we consider it as determined by the sacrifice which people are
willing to make in order to obtain it; or by
the natural and necessary conditions of its
supply; or by the elementary costs of its
production; or by the number of its producers; or by the result of all the causes of
value operating upon it, it is plain that the
labour which it will ordinarily command in
any place will measure its natural and ordinary value; and the labour which it will actually command will measure its market value.

It must always be recollected, however,
that in any sense in which we can use the
term *value of a commodity*, there must be a
reference, either expressed or implied, to some

place and time, in the same manner as when we use the term *price of a commodity.* We all well know that the price of the same kind of commodity of the same quality, weight, and dimensions, is very different in different places and at different times ; and this must be equally true in regard to the value of a commodity. It follows that, from the very nature of the thing, the value of a commodity cannot be expressed or measured independently of place and time. It is this quality which so essentially distinguishes the value of a commodity from its length or weight ; but it does not necessarily destroy its capability of being measured.

It is true, however, that a very general opinion has prevailed among political economists, even since the publication of Adam Smith's work, that from the very nature of value, so essentially different from length or weight, it cannot admit of a regular and definite measure.* This opinion seems to

* I own that I was myself for a very long time of this opinion ; but I am now perfectly convinced that I was wrong, and that Adam Smith was quite right in the

me to have arisen principally from two
causes.

First—a proper distinction has seldom
been made between the definitions of wealth
and value. Though the meanings of these
two terms have by no means always been
considered as the same, yet the characteristics
of one of them have been continually allowed

prevailing view which he took of value, though he did
not always strictly adhere to it. I am also convinced
that it would be a great improvement to the language
of political economy, if, whenever the term value, or
value in exchange, is mentioned without specific reference, it should always be understood to mean value in
exchange for labour,—the great instrument of production, and primary object given in exchange for every
thing that is wealth ; in the same manner as, when the
price of a commodity is mentioned without specific
reference, it is always understood to mean price in
money—the universal medium of exchange, and practical measure of relative value. I am further convinced
that the view of value here taken throws considerable
light on the nature of demand and the means of expressing and measuring it, and that just view of value
is absolutely necessary to a correct explanation of rents,
profits, and wages. These convictions on my mind,
which have acquired increase of strength the longer I
have considered the subject, must be my apology to
the reader for dwelling on it longer than, in considering it cursorily, he may think it deserves.

to mix themselves with the characteristics of the other. This appears even in Adam Smith himself. When he says, that a man is rich or poor according to the quantity of the necessaries, conveniencies, and luxuries of life which he can command, he gives a most correct definition of wealth; but when he afterwards says, that he is rich or poor according to the quantity of labour which he can command, he evidently confounds wealth with value. The former is a definition of wealth; and of this, or of the general power of purchasing, which too much resembles it, there is no measure. The latter is his own definition or expression of real value; and of this the very terms which he uses show that there is a measure. The measure is distinctly expressed in the terms.

The second principal cause which has prevented labour from being received, according to the language of Adam Smith, as " alone the ultimate and real standard by which the value of all commodities can at all times and places be estimated and compared,"* is,

* Wealth of Nations, b. i. c. v.

that in different periods, and in different countries, it is not really true, as stated by him, that the labourer in working. " lays down the 'same portion of his ease, his liberty, and his happiness."* There is the best reason to believe that the labourer in India, and in many other countries, neither exerts himself so much while he is working, nor works for so many hours a day as an English labourer. A day's labour, therefore, is not invariable either in regard to intensity or time. But still it appears to me that, for the reasons before stated, that is, because the labour of each place and time measures at that place and time the estimation in which a commodity is held, the state of its supply compared with the demand, the elementary costs of its production, the natural and necessary conditions of the supply, the proportion of the produce to the producers, &c. it must be considered as measuring, with a fair approach towards accuracy, the values of commodities at these places and times, so as to answer the question,—what was the value

* Wealth of Nations, b. i. c. v.

of broad-cloth of a certain description in the time of Edward III. in England? or, what is the value of money at present in China? The nature of the measure, and the reason why the varying intensity of the labour and the different number of hours employed in the day, do not disqualify it from performing its functions, may perhaps be illustrated by the following comparison:—

Let us suppose that the heights of men in different countries were extremely different, varying from six feet to six inches, and that the trees, shrubs, houses, utensils, and every other product or article were all in proportion, and that the foot-rule in each country bore the same relation to the race of human beings which inhabited it as the English foot-rule does to Englishmen: then, though it is obvious that the length of ten feet in one nation might extend over a much larger portion of space than ten feet in another nation; yet the foot of each nation would measure with accuracy the relative estimation in which men and things were held in regard to height, length, breadth, &c. It would

determine whether a man was tall or short
in the estimation of his fellow-citizens;
whether his shoulders were broad or narrow;
whether his circumference was great or
small; and not only whether Mr. Pike's nose
was longer than Mr. Chub's, but whether it
was not, in the accustomed language of the
country, absolutely a long nose, although
perhaps it might not extend to a quarter of
an English inch. On the other hand, if,
instead of referring to the measure of each
country, we were to refer always to an English
foot, though we should be able to ascertain the relative portions of space which
all the men to whom we applied our
measure occupied, we should make sad
havoc with the estimates which they and
their countrymen had formed of their own
heights, and many certainly would be considered as very short who had before always
been considered as very tall. Now it must
be allowed that the value of a commodity,
as it changes with place and time, and
depends upon the wants and caprices of
man and the means of satisfying them, re-

sembles more the estimate of tall or short, broad or narrow, than a portion of space capable of being ascertained by a measure unchangeable by time and place.

When we speak of the value of silver in China, we cannot possibly mean the value of an ounce of Chinese silver brought to London, where, if it were pure, it would be precisely of the same value as an ounce of pure silver which had been in London from time immemorial. What alone we can correctly mean is, the estimation in which the ounce of silver is held in China, determined, at the time, by the state of the supply compared with the demand, and ordinarily by the quantity of Chinese labour and profits necessary to produce it ; and if this be what we mean by the value of an ounce of silver in China, there can be no doubt that Chinese labour, and Chinese labour alone, can measure it. Even, however, if we mean the relation of an ounce of silver to all the commodities in China in succession, it would be impossible practically to form any approximation towards a just notion of the result, except by referring the silver to Chinese labour.

It might be allowed, perhaps, that labour would be a still more satisfactory measure of value, in all countries and at all times, if the physical force exerted in a day's labour were always the same; and probably this is sometimes not far from being the case in a few countries as compared with each other, and more frequently in the same country at different periods. The English agricultural labourers in the time of Edward III., though probably less skilful, worked, I should conceive, for nearly the same number of hours, and exerted nearly the same physical force, as our labourers at present. Under such circumstances, and in the same country, agricultural labour seems to be a measure of value from century to century calculated to satisfy the scruples of the most fastidious. But even when it is acknowledged, that the labourer at different times and in different countries does *not* always lay down the same portion of his ease, his liberty, and happiness, the quality of labour, as a measure of value, is not essentially impaired; and it appears to me always true, that when commodities in different countries and at different times have been found to command the same quantity of the agricultural labour of each country and time, they may with propriety be said to have been held in the same estimation, and considered as of the same value.

We may now proceed to the definition of some of the most important terms in common use among political economists, particularly those which have been most controverted. Whenever it has been thought necessary either to deviate from the general rule of employing terms according to their ordinary meaning, or to determine between two meanings both of which have some authorities in their favour, I have always been guided in my choice by what appeared to me the superior practical utility of the meaning selected in explaining the causes of the wealth of nations.*

* It is specifically on this ground that I think the meaning of the term Wealth should be confined to material objects; that productive labour should be

The reader will be aware, from the manner in which I have treated the subject, and the discussions into which I have allowed myself to enter, that what I consider as the main obstacle to a more general agreement among political economists, is rather the differences of opinion which have prevailed as to the classes of objects which are to be separated from each other by appropriate names, than as to the names which these classes should receive. It seems indeed to be pretty generally and most properly agreed, that the principal names which have been so long in use should remain. It would certainly be an Herculean task to change them, nor would any change which could be adopted in the present state of things remove the real difficulties. It has been most justly observed by Bacon, that " to say, where notions cannot be fitly reconciled, that there wanteth a

confined to that labour alone which is directly productive of wealth; and that value, or value in exchange, when no specific object is referred to, should mean value in exchange for the means of production, of which labour, the great instrument of production, is alone the representative.

term or nomenclature for it, is but a shift of
ignorance." When some people think that
every sort of gratification, whether arising
from immaterial or material objects, from spi-
ritual comfort or comfortable clothing, should
be designated by the same appropriate term ;
while others think it of great use and importance that they should be distinguished, it is
obvious that such different notions cannot be
reconciled by a new nomenclature. The grand
preliminary required is, that the notions should
be fitly reconciled ; and till this is done, a
change of names would be perfectly futile.
Preserving therefore, generally, the old
names, the great practical question is, what
they are to include and what they are to
exclude ?

Chapter X.

DEFINITIONS IN POLITICAL ECONOMY.

WEALTH.

1. THE material objects necessary, useful or agreeable to man, which have required some portion of human exertion to appropriate or produce.

UTILITY.

2. The quality of being serviceable or beneficial to mankind. The utility of an object has generally been considered as proportioned to the necessity and real importance of these services and benefits.

All wealth is necessarily useful; but all that is useful is not necessarily wealth.

VALUE,

3. Has two meanings—value in use, and value in exchange.

VALUE IN USE,

4. Is synonimous with Utility. It rarely

occurs in political economy, and is never implied by the word value when used alone.

VALUE, OR VALUE IN EXCHANGE.

5. The relation of one object to some other, or others in exchange, resulting from the estimation in which each is held. When no second object is specified, the value of a commodity naturally refers to the causes which determine this estimation, and the object which measures it.

Value is distinguished from wealth in that it is not confined to material objects, and is much more dependent upon scarcity and difficulty of production.

PRODUCTION.

6. The creation of objects which constitute wealth.

PRODUCT, PRODUCE.

7. The portion of wealth created by production.

SOURCES OF WEALTH.

8. Land, labour, and capital. The two original sources are land and labour; but the aid which labour receives from capital is

applied so very early, and is so very necessary in the production of wealth, that it may
be considered as a third source.

LAND.

9. The soil, mines, waters, and fisheries
of the habitable globe. It is the main source
of raw materials and food.

LABOUR.

10. The exertions of human beings employed with a view to remuneration. If the
term be applied to other exertions, they
must be particularly specified.

PRODUCTIVE LABOUR.

11. The labour which is so directly productive of wealth as to be capable of estimation
in the quantity or value of the products
obtained.

UNPRODUCTIVE LABOUR.

12. All labour which is not directly productive of wealth. The terms productive and
unproductive are always used by political
economists in a restricted and technical sense
exclusively applicable to the direct production or non-production of wealth.

INDUSTRY.

13. The exertion of the human faculties and powers to accomplish some desirable end. No very marked line is drawn in common language, or by political economists, between industry and labour ; but the term industry generally implies more superintendance and less bodily exertion than labour.

STOCK.

14. Accumulated wealth, either reserved by the consumer for his consumption, or kept, or employed with a view to profit.

CAPITAL.

15. That portion of the stock of a country which is kept or employed with a view to profit in the production and distribution of wealth.

FIXED CAPITAL.

16. That portion of stock employed with a view to profit which yields such profit while it remains in the possession of the owner.

CIRCULATING CAPITAL.

17. That portion of stock employed with a

view to profit which does not yield such profit till it is parted with.

REVENUE.

18. That portion of stock or wealth which the possessor may annually consume without injury to his permanent resources. It consists of the rents of land, the wages of labour, and the profits of stock.

ACCUMULATION OF CAPITAL.

19. The employment of a portion of revenue as capital. Capital may therefore increase without an increase of stock or wealth.

SAVING,

20. In modern times, implies the accumulation of capital, as few people now lock up their money in a box.

RENT OF LAND.

21. That portion of the produce of land which remains to the owner after all the outgoings belonging to its cultivation are paid, including the ordinary profits of the capital employed.

MONEY-RENT OF LAND.

22. The average rent of land as before defined, estimated in money.

GROSS SURPLUS OF THE LAND.

23. That portion of the produce of land which is not actually consumed by the cultivators.

WAGES OF LABOUR.

24. The remuneration paid to the labourer for his exertions.

NOMINAL WAGES.

25. The wages which the labourer receives in the current money of the country.

REAL WAGES.

26. The necessaries, conveniencies, and luxuries of life which the wages of the labourer enable him to command.

THE RATE OF WAGES.

27. The ordinary wages paid to the labourer by the day, week, month, or year, according to the custom of the place where he is employed. They are generally estimated in money.

.THE PRICE OF LABOUR,

28. Has generally been understood to mean the average money-price of common day-labour, and is not therefore different from the rate of wages, except that it more specifically refers to money.

THE AMOUNT OF WAGES.

29. The whole earnings of the labourer in a given time, which may be much more or much less than the average rate of wages, or the price of common day-labour.

THE PRICE OF EFFECTIVE LABOUR.

30. The price in money of a given quantity of human exertion of a given strength and character, which may be essentially different from the common price of day-labour, or the whole money-earnings of the labourer in a given time.

ACCUMULATED LABOUR.

31. The labour worked up in the raw materials and tools applied to the production of other commodities.

PROFITS OF STOCK.

32. When stock is employed as capital in

the production and distribution of wealth, its profits consist of the difference between the value of the capital advanced, and the value of the commodity when sold or used.

THE RATE OF PROFITS.

33. The per centage proportion which the value of the profits upon any capital bears to the value of such capital.

THE INTEREST OF MONEY.

34. The net profits of a capital in money separated from the risk and trouble of employing it.

THE PROFITS OF INDUSTRY, SKILL, AND ENTERPRISE.

35. That portion of the gross profits of capital, independent of monopoly, which remains after deducting the net profits, or the interest of money.

MONOPOLY PROFITS.

36. The profits which arise from the employment of capital where the competition is not free.

CONDITIONS OF THE SUPPLY OF COMMODITIES.

37. The advance of the quantity of accumulated and immediate labour necessary to their production, with such a per centage upon the whole of the advances for the time they have been employed as is equivalent to ordinary profits. If there be any other necessary conditions of the supply arising from monopolies of any description, or from taxes, they must be added.

ELEMENTARY COSTS OF PRODUCTION.

38. An expression exactly equivalent to the conditions of the supply.

MEASURE OF THE CONDITIONS OF THE SUPPLY, OR OF THE ELEMENTARY COSTS OF PRODUCTION.

39. The quantity of labour for which the commodity will exchange, when it is in its natural and ordinary state.

THE VALUE, MARKET VALUE, OR ACTUAL VALUE, OF A COMMODITY AT ANY PLACE OR TIME.

40. The estimation in which it is held at that place and time, determined in all cases

by the state of the supply compared with the demand, and ordinarily by the elementary costs of production which regulate that state.

THE NATURAL VALUE OF A COMMODITY AT ANY PLACE AND TIME.

41. The estimation in which it is held when it is in its natural and ordinary state, determined by the elementary costs of its production, or the conditions of its supply.

MEASURE OF THE MARKET OR ACTUAL VALUE OF A COMMODITY AT ANY PLACE OR TIME.

42. The quantity of labour which it will command or exchange for at that place and time.

MEASURE OF THE NATURAL VALUE OF A COMMODITY AT ANY PLACE AND TIME.

43. The quantity of labour for which it will exchange at that place and time, when it is in its natural and ordinary state.

THE PRICE, THE MARKET PRICE, OR ACTUAL PRICE OF A COMMODITY AT ANY PLACE AND TIME.

44. The quantity of money for which it

exchanges at that place and time, the money referring to the precious metals.

THE NATURAL PRICE OF A COMMODITY AT ANY PLACE AND TIME.

45. The price in money which will pay the elementary costs of its production, or the money conditions of its supply.

SUPPLY OF COMMODITIES

46. The quantity offered, or ready to be immediately offered, for sale.

DEMAND FOR COMMODITIES,

47. Has two distinct meanings : one, in regard to its extent, or the quantity of commodities purchased ; and the other, in regard to its intensity, or the sacrifice which the demanders are able and willing to make in order to satisfy their wants.

DEMAND IN REGARD TO ITS EXTENT.

48. The quantity of the commodity purchased, which generally increases with the increase of the supply, and diminishes with the diminution of it. It is often the greatest when commodities are selling below the costs of production.

DEMAND IN REGARD TO ITS INTENSITY.

49. The sacrifice which the demanders are able and willing to make in order to satisfy their wants. It is this species of demand alone which, compared with the supply, determines prices and values.

EFFECTUAL DEMAND, IN REGARD TO ITS EXTENT.

50. The quantity of a commodity wanted by those who are able and willing to pay the costs of its production.

EFFECTUAL DEMAND, IN REGARD TO ITS INTENSITY.

51. The sacrifice which the demanders must make, in order to effectuate the continued supply of a commodity.

MEASURE OF THE INTENSITY OF THE EFFECTUAL DEMAND.

52. The quantity of labour for which the commodity will exchange, when in its natural and ordinary state.

EXCESS OF THE DEMAND ABOVE THE SUPPLY.

53. The demand for a commodity is said

to be in excess above the supply, when, either from the diminution of the supply, or the increase of the effectual demand, the quantity in the market is not sufficient to supply all the effectual demanders. In this case the intensity of the demand increases, and the commodity rises, in proportion to the competition of the demanders, and the sacrifice they are able and willing to make in order to satisfy their wants.

EXCESS OF THE SUPPLY ABOVE THE DEMAND, OR PARTIAL GLUT.

54. The supply of a commodity is said to be in excess above the demand, or there is a partial glut, when, either from the superabundance of supply, or the diminution of demand, the quantity in the market exceeds the quantity wanted by those who are able and willing to pay the elementary costs of production. It then falls below these costs in proportion to the eagerness of the sellers to sell; and the glut is trifling, or great, accordingly.

GENERAL GLUT.

55. A glut is said to be general, when, either from superabundance of supply or diminution of demand, a considerable mass of commodities falls below the elementary costs of production.

A GIVEN DEMAND.

56. A given demand, in regard to price, is a given quantity of money intended to be laid out in the purchase of certain commodities in a market; and a given demand, in regard to value, is the command of a given quantity of labour intended to be employed in the same way.

VARIATIONS OF PRICES AND VALUES.

57. Prices and values vary as the demand directly and the supply inversely. When the demand is given, prices and values vary inversely as the supply; when the supply is given, directly as the demand.

CONSUMPTION.

58. The destruction wholly or in part of any portions of wealth.

PRODUCTIVE CONSUMPTION.

59. The consumption or employment of wealth by the capitalist, with a view to future production.

UNPRODUCTIVE CONSUMPTION, OR SPENDING.

60. The consumption of wealth, as revenue, with a view to the final purpose of all production—subsistence and enjoyment; but not with a view to profit.

———

CHAPTER XI.

OBSERVATIONS ON THE DEFINITIONS.

Def. 1. THE reader will be aware that, in almost all definitions, the same meaning may be conveyed in different language, and that it is the meaning rather than the mode of expressing it that should be the main object of our consideration. The essential question in the definition of wealth is, whether or not it should be confined to material objects, and the reader is already apprised of my reasons for thinking that it should. Even M. Say, who admits " *les produits immatériels,*" allows, as I have before stated (p. 93), that the multiplication of them " *ne fait rien pour la richesse ;*" and M. Storch, in his able " *Cours d'Economie Politique,*" though he justly lays great stress on what he calls *les biens internes,* with a view to civilization and the indirect production of wealth, confines the term *richesses* to *biens externes,* or material objects ; and according to this meaning treats of the *Théorie de la Richesse Nationale*, in the first, and far the largest, part of his work. Altogether, I can feel no doubt that some classification of this kind, or some separation of material from immaterial objects is, in the highest degree, useful in a definition of wealth.

The latter part of the definition is of minor importance. It is intended to exclude such material objects as air, light, rain, &c.—which, however necessary and useful to man, are seldom considered as wealth ; and, perhaps, it is more objectionable to exclude them, by the introduction of the term exchangeable value into a definition of wealth, than in the mode which has been adopted. If the latter clause were not added, the only consequence would be, that, in comparing different countries together, such objects as air, light, &c., would be neglected as common quantities.

Def. 2. I have already alluded to the manner in which M. Say has applied the term Utility. His language cannot be considered as consistent, when he says that the price of an article is the measure of its utility, although it might be, according to his own expression, *la chose la plus inutile.** It is much better for the science of political economy that the term should retain its natural and ordinary meaning. All wealth is no doubt useful, but there are so very many immaterial, and some material objects which are highly useful, and yet not wealth, that there can be no excuse for confounding them. M. Storch has not escaped the same kind of error.

Def. 5. Two articles are never exchanged with each other without a previous estimation being formed of the value of each, by a reference to the wants of mankind and the means of production. This general and most important relation to the means of production, and the labour which represents these means, seems to be quite forgotten by those who imagine that there is no relation implied

* Traité d'Economie Politique, Epitome, vol. ii. p. 506, 4th edit.

when the value of a commodity is mentioned without specific reference to some other commodity.

M. Say, under the head *Valeur des Choses*, observes, " c'est la quantité d'autres choses évaluables qu'on peut obtenir en échange d'elle."* This is a most vague and uncertain definition, and much less satisfactory than the general power of purchasing.

M. Storch says, that " la valeur des choses c'est leur utilité relative;" but this certainly cannot be said unless we completely change the natural and ordinary meaning either of utility or value.

Neither M. Say nor M. Storch has sufficiently distinguished utility, wealth, and value.

Def. 6. The term creation is not here meant to apply to the creation of matter, but to the creation and production of the objects which have been defined to be wealth.

Defs. 11 *and* 12. If wealth be confined to material objects, it must be allowed to be

* Epitome, vol. ii. p. 507.

peculiarly convenient and useful, in explaining
the causes of the wealth of nations, to have
some appropriate term for that species of
labour which directly produces wealth ; and as
the principal founder of the science of political economy has used the terms *productive
labour* in the restricted sense necessary for
this special purpose, perhaps few objections
would have been made to it, if it had not
involved all other kinds of labour, however
useful and important, under the apparently
disparaging designation of unproductive. This
is a consequence, no doubt, to be regretted :
yet, when it has been repeatedly stated that
the term unproductive, as applied by Adam
Smith, in no degree impeaches the utility and
importance of such labour, but merely implies
that it does not directly produce gross wealth,
the mere name ought not to decide against a
classification for which it appears from experience that it is very difficult to find a
satisfactory substitute.

In M. Storch's " *Considérations sur la
Nature du Revenu National,*" he does not
appear to me to give a correct view of what

Adam Smith means by productive labour.*
The difficulty of classification above alluded
to appears strikingly in this treatise. There
is some plausibility in the system, and
it is explained with ingenuity and ability;
but I think that the adoption of it would
destroy all precision in the science of political economy.

Defs. 19 *and* 20. I have never been able
to understand how the accumulation of capital
and the difference between saving and spending can be distinctly explained, if we call all
labour equally productive.

Def. 23. It is this gross surplus of the
land which furnishes the means of subsistence
to the inhabitants of towns and cities. Besides
the rents of land, which are powerfully effective in this respect, a large part of what,
in the division of the produce of land, would
fall to the shares of the farmers and labourers,
is exchanged by them for other objects of
convenience and gratification, thus giving the

* c. iv. p. 83.

main necessaries of life to a great mass of persons not immediately connected with the soil. The proportion which this mass of persons may bear to the cultivators will depend upon the natural fertility of the soil, and the skill with which it has been improved, and continues to be worked.

Defs. 28 *and* 30. In a valuable publication on the *Price of Corn, and Wages of Labour,* by Sir Edward West, which has just fallen into my hands, he proposes that the *price of labour* should mean the sum paid for a given quantity of labour of a given character. I quite agree with him in thinking that it would be useful to have some appropriate term to express this meaning; but, as the *price of labour* has certainly not hitherto been used in this sense, and as it would be, in almost all cases, extremely difficult to give an answer to a question respecting the price of labour so understood, it would certainly be proper to vary the expression in some degree, in order to prepare people for a new meaning. In

Definition 30, therefore, I have given this meaning to *The price of effective labour.*

Def. 31. It would save time and circumlocution, which is one of the great objects of appropriate terms, if, in speaking of the labour worked up in commodities, the labour worked up in the capital necessary to their production were designated by the term *accumulated labour,* as contradistinguished from the *immediate labour* employed by the last capitalist. We must always recollect, however, that labour is not the only element worked up in capital.—

Def. 38. I have used the word *elementary,* in order to show that money-costs are not meant. On account of the doubt which may arise in this respect when the term *costs of production* is used alone, and the further doubt, whether ordinary profits are always included, I am decidedly of opinion that *the conditions of the supply* is a more expressive and less uncertain term for the same meaning. I do not find, however, that generally it is so well understood. I have defined, therefore, *the costs of production* with the addition of the word *elementary*, and including profits, as having precisely the same meaning as the conditions of the supply. I once thought it might be better not to include profits in costs of production ; but as Adam Smith has included them, and more particularly as the profits worked up in the capital necessary to any production must form a part of the advances or *costs* in any sense in which the word costs can be used, I think it best, on the whole, to include necessary pro fits in the elementary costs of production. They are obviously included in the necessary conditions of the supply.

Defs. 39 *and* 40. In speaking of the quantity of labour for which a commodity will exchange, as a measure either of the conditions of its supply or of its value, it must always be understood, that the different kinds of labour which may have been employed to produce it, must be reduced to labour of one description and of the lowest denomination, namely, common agricultural day-labour, estimated on an average throughout the year. This is the kind of labour which is always referred to when labour is spoken of as a measure.

Def. 57. It is not true, as stated by M. Say, that prices rise in the direct ratio of the *quantity* demanded, and the inverse ratio of the *quantity* supplied.* They only vary in this way, when the demand is understood to mean the sacrifice which the demanders are able and willing to make, in order to supply themselves with what they want; which may be represented in regard to price by the quantity of money ready to be employed in purchases in a market. When the demand for *labour* is spoken of, it can only relate to *extent;* and a greater demand can only signify a power of commanding a greater *quantity* of labour.

Def. 59. The only productive consumption, properly so called, is the consumption

* Vol. ii. p. 17. 4th edition.

or destruction of wealth by capitalists with a view to reproduction. This is the only marked line of distinction which can be drawn between productive and unproductive consumption. The workman whom the capitalist employs certainly consumes that part of his wages which he does not save, as revenue, with a view to subsistence and enjoyment; and not as capital, with a view to production. He is a productive consumer to the person who employs him, and to the state, but not, strictly speaking, to himself. Consumption is the great purpose and end of all production. The consumption of wealth, as revenue, with a view to support and enjoyment, is even more necessary and important than the consumption of wealth as capital ; but their effects are essentially different in regard to the direct production of wealth, and they ought therefore to be distinguished.

I AM far from meaning to present the fore-
going definitions to the notice of the reader
as in any degree complete, either in regard
to extent, or correctness. In extent, they
have been purposely limited, and in regard
to correctness, I am too well aware of the
difficulty of the subject to think that I have
succeeded in making my definitions embrace
all I wish, and exclude all I wish. I am
strongly, indeed, disposed to believe, that in
the sciences of morals, politics, and political
economy, which will not admit of a change
in the principal terms already in use, the
full attainment of this object is impossible;
yet a nearer approach to it is always something gained. I should not indeed have been
justified in offering these definitions to the
public, if I had not thought that they were,
on the whole, less objectionable, and would
be more useful in explaining the causes of
the wealth of nations than any which I had
seen. But I am conscious of some anomalies,
and probably there are some more of which
I am not conscious. Knowing, however, that

the attempt to remove them might destroy useful classifications, I shall not consider a few individual cases, of little importance, as valid objections.

It is known that Adam Smith gave few regular definitions; but the meanings in which he used his terms may be collected from the context, and to these I have, in a considerable degree, adhered. For some I have been indebted to M. Say; others are my own; and in all, I have endeavoured to follow the rules for the definition and use of terms laid down at the beginning of this treatise. I shall consider my object as fully answered, if what I have done, should succeed in drawing that degree of attention to the subject which may lead to the production of something of the same kind, more correct and more useful, and so convincing as to be generally adopted.